Augustine,
a Mother's Son

Dolina MacCuish

Christian Focus

To my parents
Roderick and Elizabeth

© Dolina MacCuish
ISBN 1 85792 437 1
Published in 1999
by
Christian Focus Publications,
Geanies House, Fearn, Ross-shire,
IV20 1TW, Great Britain.

Contents

Introduction

'What women these Christians have!' exclaimed the pagan orator, Libanius, and no wonder if Monica is anything to go by.

The relationship between her and her younger son is of the stuff in which the psychologist in us revels – for the information we are given (though largely from one side) is just enough to intrigue while still leaving open questions. Hence the fascination.

Equally fascinating is the startling frankness with which Augustine examines the 'labyrinthine ways' of his own mind as he fled Him 'down the arches of the years' who in mercy followed after.

All in all, it is a story of hope – for all of us but especially, perhaps, for weeping (and praying) mothers everywhere.

Chapter 1

Monica

Fifteen years after sailing from his native Africa Augustine described how, in the early morning light, his mother stood on the pier at Carthage in a frenzy of grief. For a long time she stood scarcely aware in her anguish of the milling life around her – the little boats criss-crossing the harbour, the clatter and clang of vessels mooring or casting off, the shouts of the dockers as they loaded the grain-ships. She had done all in her power to stop him – had even followed him to the waterside determined that they should not be parted. In a nearby chapel she had spent the night in prayer imploring God to prevent him, somehow, from sailing. Now he was gone.

She had good cause for her fears – perils over sea and perils over land were as nothing to the nameless, unfocused dangers of an unknown city (and not physical dangers alone). And, more, there was the manner of his going. As the complex of emotions swept over her she broke into wild cries and sobbing as she bitterly charged him with his treachery and cruelty.

Then, defeated and alone, she turned to the only help she knew and, as so often before, poured out her heart to God for him. So many prayers, so many tears.......

The bustling port of Carthage held no attraction for Monica so it is likely that within a few days she was setting out on the 200-mile journey southwestwards to her home town of Thagaste.

Thagaste (modern Souk Ahras in Algeria) was a small town of some few thousand inhabitants in that part of North Africa once known as Numidia. It lay sixty miles south of the Mediterranean coast and two hundred feet above sea level and had already been in existence for three hundred years. The name is Latin for it was one of many such Roman towns dotted throughout the province. By the late fourth century all the lands round the Mediterranean – Greece, Turkey, Asia Minor, Spain, France and North Africa – belonged to the Roman Empire. Thagaste was the sort of place where everybody knew everybody and Monica had her own very special and honoured place there. It was where she belonged.

There she had been born about AD 330 into what seems to have been (for Thagaste) a relatively well-to-do family. Hers was a Christian home and it would appear that she readily followed the teaching and ideals that she learned there. Her son was later to record, 'It was by Christ's teaching, by the guidance of Thine only Son, that she was brought up to honour and obey Thee in one of those good Christian families which form the body of Thy church,' adding, 'but she was made subject rather by Thee to her parents than by her parents to Thee.'

The upbringing of the children was largely in the hands of an old servant who had been with the family for many years. They listened enthralled to her stories of 'the olden days' when their father was a little boy and she used to carry him about pick-a-back. Now she was old and not as nimble as she once had been but she was wise and sensible and dependable – just the person to be entrusted with the moral guidance of the girls. She seems to have had a fairly free hand and took her duties seriously. We are given a glimpse of her methods. The only time she would allow them to drink water was at meal-times when children and parents sat down together. Otherwise drinking was forbidden even when they were parched with thirst. When they asked the reason for this she would tell them, 'It's to keep you from developing a bad habit. You drink water now because you have no access to wine but when you are married and have the key of cellar and cupboard, you will turn up your nose at water, but the habit of drinking will remain.' There is a certain odd logic in it!

What actually happened threatened to subvert her plan long before those heady days. Her parents took to sending the sober little Monica down to the cellar to fetch wine. On one occasion, while engaged in her important task, she drew the wine from the cask into a cup as usual and was about to pour it into the flagon when she raised it to her lips and sipped the tiniest drop, just for the fun of it. It was nice to be on her own – no grown-ups about. Next trip to the cellar led to two little sips and so it went on day by day till eventually she was drinking off her noggin almost full to the brim. The nurse's theory wasn't working out too well in practice!

Where it might have ended we know not. Fortunately it happened that one day Monica had a quarrel with the young maid who was in the habit of accompanying her to the cellar.

The war of words escalated into the inevitable name-calling. Back and forth the epithets flew till the girl gave the *coup de grâce*. 'Well, look at you; you're just an alcoholic. I see you. Every time you're sent for wine you ....' The arrow found its target and that was the end of the wine-tasting.

The old servant who took such an interest in the moral education of her young charges was a devout Christian and her example and teaching played a crucial role in the formation of the young girl's character and convictions. By this time Christianity was widespread in North Africa, coexisting with the indigenous religions and the paganism of Rome but when Monica was given in marriage it was not to a fellow-Christian, as might have been expected, but to a pagan, Patricius Herculus.

As she had been a good, obedient daughter Monica now set out to be a good, obedient wife. Marriage between a pagan and a practising Christian would almost guarantee some tension, underlying if not overt, what with differences of lifestyle, expectations, and ideals, and so it proved.

Added to which there was, in the early days, friction between the young bride and her mother-in-law due mainly to the malicious gossip of the servants. Monica had need of patience and as much tact as she could muster. She went cheerfully and doggedly on with her duties so that in time the older woman began to suspect that she was being deliberately misled and brought the matter up with Patricius. There was quite a showdown. It was, his mother pointed out, he who had engaged these mischief-makers as servants in the first place and, furthermore, as head of the house it was up to him to sort them out. Patricius promptly obliged, laying about him vigorously with blows and slaps all round while mother-in-law let it be known that there would be more of the same for any who henceforth should miscall her daughter. And so they lived ever after 'in the utmost sweetness and goodwill' as Monica recollected.

Clearly Patricius was not a man to brook contradiction for though in some respects he was generous and easy-going, he had a quick temper. Monica refused to argue, especially when he was not quite sober – but when he had cooled down she would calmly help him to see that she had been right after all! Her sweet reasonableness won his admiration but did not stop him being unfaithful. Monica never complained but not from indifference;

she had her reasons. She may or may not have had in mind the apostle Peter's injunction to wives so to conduct themselves that their unbelieving husbands might be won over by their example, but she acted in accordance with it. So there was harmony of a sort between the two.

Neighbours and friends were more than a little puzzled. Patricius was known for his short temper yet his wife seemed not to suffer – no tell-tale signs of beatings, never a rumour of rows. They talked about it among themselves. Some of them had husbands who were a lot milder than Patricius yet too often their bruised faces told a story of violence. When they exchanged confidences and asked Monica to let them into her secret she would laugh:

'Well girls, we're servants you know – the marriage contract as good as says so. When you heard it read out you should have said to yourself, "That's my new job – servant to his lordship!" You've got to remember that and not quarrel with your master. That's the secret – knowing our place!'

They'd laugh with her but knew that Monica meant it. Some took her advice and thanked her – it worked! Others could not bring themselves to do so and continued to suffer. Indubitably a man's world – though the women generally held the purse-strings!

Monica was a wise and kindly neighbour, tactful and peace-loving. When they came to her with their complaints (the two parties in a dispute frequently confiding in her about the other), she made a point of relating only what would be a help towards reconciliation.

In time three, possibly four, children were added to the family; a son, Navigius, followed by a daughter, Perpetua (and perhaps a second daughter) and then on the Lord's Day, 13 November 354, the boy who would put the sleepy little town of Thagaste on the map of the world for all time. Monica was twenty-three years old when Aurelius Augustinus was born.

Chapter 2

Roman Africa

The world into which Augustine was born had about it a deceptive air of permanence and stability. He probably belonged, at least on his mother's side, to the Berber race, one of the oldest in the world and the origins of which are lost in the mists of time. Variously described as short and swarthy or pale-skinned, fair-haired and blue-eyed they are noted for their independent spirit, vitality and force of personality. They have always maintained a distinctive way of life though they have never been organised into a state, nor have they ever been completely assimilated by their conquerors.

When Phoenician traders and explorers arrived in 1200 BC Berbers already occupied North Africa and there is still a large population of them in that area. The invaders had been establishing colonies all around the Mediterranean, gradually extending their influence till they became undisputed masters of the sea. According to tradition Carthage was founded by Queen Dido of Tyre in 814 BC and two centuries later had become the centre of a great trading republic. The Berber peoples adopted such aspects of their culture as appealed to them but, true to form, retained their independence.

Another major force in Africa was Rome. Founded in the eighth century BC on its seven hills by the River Tiber it had by the third century BC become a republic and, having expanded into Asia and Eastern Europe, was already casting acquisitive eyes across the sea to Africa. It took one hundred and fifty years and three Punic wars for the Romans to achieve their ambition. It was in an attempt to throw off the Roman threat once and for all that Hannibal, the resourceful Carthaginian general, engaged in the brave and imaginative feat of leading 40,000 men and some thirty elephants across the Straits of Gibraltar into Spain and over the Alps to launch a surprise attack on the enemy. The Romans, terrified by the living tanks bearing down on them, lost fifty thousand men in one battle but lived to fight another day and finally, in 146 BC, Carthage was burned to the ground and Rome was master in North Africa. The Romans alluded to the Berbers as *barbari*, barbarians, and the name stuck but, significantly, they called themselves *Amazigh*, free men.

Under Roman rule, Africa had prospered economically and was exporting so much grain that it was known as the breadbasket of Rome. It was a land of small farmers. Grapes and olives, with their associated wine and oil industries, were also extensively cultivated. The need for receptacles for the olive oil generated a thriving pottery works. There was a brisk export trade in textiles (especially the much-coveted purple cloth), animal skins and live animals in their thousands; these last to keep the gladiatorial shows supplied. In Numidia was quarried the yellow marble (*giallo antico*) used in so many Roman buildings. Thousands of camels carried this bounty to the waiting ships on the coast.

Good straight roads, mostly unpaved in the countryside, linked the many towns and provided quick and easy access to the Mediterranean ports. To the south a string of fortresses guarded the frontier on the northern edge of the Sahara. Numerous ruins, some remarkably well-preserved, bear testimony to this day to the building skills and energy of the Romans. Perhaps one of the most impressive is the amphitheatre at El Djem, dwarfing the modern town and with a capacity of thirty thousand. The theatre at Dougga is still used when the occasion warrants it. Excavations at Bulla Regia, built by the toil of 50,000 slaves, have revealed several villas with intrically-worked mosaic floors and an impressive baths.

Even today the Roman gods and goddesses are part and parcel of the imagination and culture of the western world: our very languages bear witness to them. Most human attributes and activities had their deities – Mars the god of war, Venus the goddess of love, Mercury the winged messenger and a thousand more – and the stories about them are legion. It was important to placate them if you had reason to fear that you had offended them. Religion was the business of the state which saw to the building of huge statues of the gods, and temples in their honour. Religious observances were for the most part left to the priests although there were also household gods. Meanwhile many Carthaginians and Berbers continued to honour their own deities, sometimes under Roman names.

It is difficult for those in a Christian land to appreciate that there was no moral content whatsoever in Roman religion. The gods were made in the image of men with all-too-human passions and failings. Not that the Romans were without a moral code; they had moral ideals, especially in the early years, but these did not derive from their religion. A passion for liberty, justice and virtue surely accounts in part for their achievements.

By the fourth century AD, therefore, the three provinces of North Africa had been under Roman rule for five centuries and it must have seemed as if this state of affairs was set to continue. These three provinces were Mauretania (now Morocco and western Algeria), Numidia (eastern Algeria and western Tunisia) and Africa (eastern Tunisia and Libya). Though the Roman culture was dominant, Punic customs and language lingered on, especially along the coast, while in the country districts inland the Berber dialects continued to be spoken.

Then to the Berber, Punic and Roman culture and religion was added the influence of Christianity. In 55 BC, as every schoolboy once knew, Julius Caesar came to Britain, that land on the world's edge. His great-nephew, Augustus, became the first Emperor and it was during his reign that, in a far-flung corner of the Empire, the child Jesus was born. Rome's attitude to other religions was in general tolerant; provided they were not troublesome Rome was not greatly interested. After all, when there was some agitation among the Jews regarding Jesus of Nazareth, the Roman Governor, Pilate, wanted to wash his hands of the whole affair, though he finally succumbed to the demands of the mob and Christ was crucified.

After His resurrection Christ commissioned his disciples to spread the good news throughout the world, 'beginning at Jerusalem', and three hundred years later Christianity was well established in Africa despite sporadic and severe outbreaks of persecution on account of the Christians' refusal to worship the Emperor. Tertullian, living in Carthage at the beginning of the third century mocked the persecutors; 'If the Tiber overflows and reaches the walls, or the Nile refuses to overflow and flood the fields, if the clouds do not move or the earth does, if there is famine or pestilence the cry is at once: "The Christians to the lion!" What! All to one lion?' When Constantine defeated his rival, Maxentius, at Milvian Bridge in 312 to become Emperor he attributed his victory to the Christians' God for during the battle had he not seen a cross in the sky with the words, 'BY THIS SIGN WIN'? The Edict of Milan in the following year granted toleration to Christian and pagan alike and by mid-century Christianity was recognised as the official religion of the Empire. In Africa, despite accretions and distortions that had no authorisation from the Scriptures, a robust Christianity struggled and grew.

So in society at large there was a ferment of ideas and ideals. The children in the home at Thagaste felt the tug of these currents and cross-currents in their lives for there they were reflected in miniature.

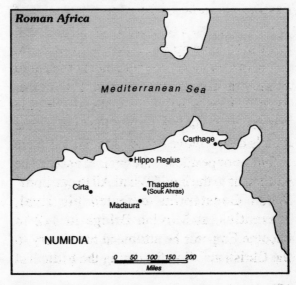

Chapter 3

Boyhood

By the mid-fourth century AD, had they but known it, the heyday of the Empire was past – that Empire that still seemed so permanent and unshakeable. The very buildings that sat so solid and strong seemed to announce, 'We're here to stay' and indeed many of them have endured. The seeds of disintegration were as yet barely discernible except perhaps to the more perceptive. Change and decay were working to bring the *Pax Romana* to an end but as yet the portents were no bigger than the size of a man's hand.

But to the little boy roaming the countryside around Thagaste with his brother and friends questions about the rise and fall of empires were of little import. The high wide landscape, ever-changing according to the season of the year, bright with an abundance of wild flowers in spring, tawny in the dry season, crisp and cold in the short winter, was empire and world to him.

Monica did her best to instil Christian

principles. When they were born she had the children blessed with the sign of the cross and given salt in token of her intention to bring them up 'in the fear and admonition of the Lord.' In this she succeeded to the extent that all in the home accounted themselves Christians – except Patricius who remained a pagan but apparently did not object to Monica's influence over the children. So Augustine was taught the basic moral outlook of Christianity and understood and appreciated (up to a point!) his mother's interest in his moral and spiritual development. Over and over in his writings he refers to her prayers on behalf of her children and her tears when they went astray. He noticed her twice-daily visits to church, her conscientious almsgiving, her readiness to help any who were in trouble and how on saints' days she would carry her little basket of cakes and bread to the shrine of the saint whose commemoration it was. There she would taste the bread as a sign of devotion and encourage others by sharing with them the bread and wine.

That the boy took his mother's teaching seriously is indicated by an incident that happened while he was a young child. He came home one day complaining of a severe pain in his stomach. Soon he was running a temperature and tossing and turning in a high fever. Nothing seemed to help. Afraid he was about to die, he pleaded with his mother to let him be baptised. Monica, anxious to make the right decision, was busy making the necessary arrangements when the invalid suddenly took a turn for the better and went on to make a full recovery. His baptism was promptly deferred according to custom. The view had come about that baptism washed away one's past sins and that sins after baptism entailed greater guilt, so it was thought expedient to delay the rite: hence Monica's initial hesitation.

As for his father, Augustine seldom mentions him in his autobiography. However, that is primarily an account of his spiritual odyssey and there it was his mother's influence that was paramount. While it would not be wise to read too much into silence, he did feel that his father had failed to understand him as a person and certainly took no interest in his moral or spiritual well-being. 'He saw only what was on the surface as far as I was concerned,' he reminisced. It may be that his mother's apparently excessive subservience (discretion being the better part of valour?) bred in him a resentment towards his father.

He frankly says that his mother was much the better of the two and that she encouraged them to look to God as their father rather than to him.

Patricius was evidently well-respected by his fellow-townsmen, being a member of the town council. Under the Empire there were no ethnic barriers and it was open to anyone who was free (that is, not a slave) to become a full member of a Roman town. Like most of his neighbours he would work his little plot of land outside the town and made a sufficient living though there was never much to spare and Augustine remembered being poorly dressed.

Augustine's verdict on his childhood was that even if he had lived to boyhood only, he would have reason to thank God for 'I was, I lived, I felt .... I learned to delight in truth, to enquire minutely into things; I hated to be deceived, had a good memory, could express myself well, enjoyed my friends, shrank from pain and had a thirst for knowledge.' It was a happy life for a boy, with ball games and bird-hunting in summer, the chance of a snow-fight in winter, raiding the cupboards at home for booty with which to coax his friends to come playing with him (not that they needed bribing!), cheating to win and then hotly denying it. But if he caught anyone cheating .... 'So small a boy, so great a sinner,' he recalled, adding that in the adult world these very sins persist, except that 'nuts and balls and sparrows become gold, mansions and slaves while tutors and teachers are replaced by magistrates and kings.'

There was always something to engage his attention – swallows, storks and doves building their nests, a lizard catching flies, or a spider entangling them in her web. There was the whole fascinating world of insects and small creatures – mice, beetles, bees, locusts, worms, frogs – to explore. The day was never long enough and like children the world over, how he grudged to hear the bedtime call! And always in the background the sounds of men at work in the fields singing and calling to one another as they tilled the fertile earth, or sowed and harvested their crops of grain or fruit beneath wide skies full of light.

Then school intervened.

Chapter 4

The Happiest Days?

Monica and Patricius, divided in so many ways, were agreed about one thing – the value of education; so off to school Augustine was sent 'to get learning in which (*miserere mei!*) I knew not what use there was,' he recalled. He hated it!

For one thing there were the dreaded beatings – an integral part of one's education it seemed. And it was no use looking to the grown-ups for sympathy; they only laughed. These beatings worried him – but what to do about them? If tears and prayers availed for mothers then why not for boys sore beset by the hazards of life? To his tears he therefore added prayers – fervent, urgent prayers – but all in vain and a good thing too, he reflected, for if ever a boy deserved what he got, he did – skipping classes to play with his friends or sneaking off to shows and inventing stories to cover up their misdeeds. 'Our sole delight was play and for this we were punished by those who were doing the same themselves – only

27

the grown-ups called their idleness business!'
When word of their escapades reached
Monica's ears she was driven to even more
earnest prayers and tears, which no doubt made
Augustine feel bad, for a time at least.

The floggings were unbearable, the lessons
not much better. Maths he detested. 'To chant,

"One and one make two,

Two and two make four!"

I loathed the very sound of it.' Kicking a
ball around was much more to his liking than
this.

Then there was Greek. 'Not one word of it
did I understand, even though urged on by
fierce threats and punishments.' He never did
master the language nor could he ever fathom
why, exactly, he hated it so much.

Now Latin was a different matter. Latin he
loved – not the business of reading and writing
as such, for that was as bad as any Greek, but
the literature. The myths and legends appealed
to, and enriched, his vivid imagination. He
thrilled to the story of the wooden horse of
Troy. (What schoolboy doesn't?) Latin he had
learned at his mother's knee and probably
spoke at home. No one had tried to beat Latin
into him. Rather it was praise and smiles all
round at his first attempts to form words. That

is how learning should be, he concluded, unconstrained and spontaneous. Curiosity is a better spur than coercion and fear.

Boring or not, he came to regard what he learned in the school at Thagaste – basically the three Rs – as more worthwhile and useful than much of his subsequent education.

* * * * * * * * * *

By his early teens the school at Thagaste had taken him as far as it could and, as he was now eager to learn and obviously a bright boy, his parents determined to give him the best education they could. Money had to be found to pay his fees and this entailed some scrimping and saving which they willingly undertook. Patricius proved himself a good father in this respect, rightly winning the admiration of his fellow-citizens; many of them were much better off than he but took little interest in their sons' education.

So off he set on the twenty mile journey across the river and on and up to the university town of Madaura in order to attend the grammar school there. Madaura lay to the south-west of Thagaste and was built according to the grid pattern of most Roman towns. Around the Forum were ranged the public buildings including the pagan temples and the town hall with the law courts. Nearby were situated the theatre, library and public baths with statues, triumphal arches or monuments to the mighty gracing every corner. The ruins of the basilica may still be seen as may parts of the road over which Augustine travelled.

Although it was a pagan education that he was to receive, Monica had no misgivings for she took the view that not only was it the route to success but it would, she hoped and constantly prayed, equip him to be, in time, a better Christian. The curriculum was purely language-based, the aim being to produce a highly articulate speaker since mastery of the spoken word was the key to influence and power, opening the door to a career in the civil service or law. Students learned how to present information effectively, to deploy argument, to persuade, to play on the listeners' emotions, and to ensure that they enjoyed every minute of it. To that end they employed all the verbal pyrotechnics at their command – epigram, pun, simile, metaphor, the lot. Every word was important. Terence, Cicero, Virgil and Tacitus, to name a few, were studied in such detail that substantial parts of their works would be known by heart. The teacher went over the text sentence by sentence, word by word, explicating it and drawing out every last nuance of meaning and significance.

Those thus educated formed part of a cultural élite who understood one another across geographical and cultural boundaries. A word or phrase could evoke in the hearer a whole context and world of meaning and allusion, much as a phrase from the Bible or Shakespeare could do in the English-speaking world at certain periods in its history.

Augustine did well at school. He won a prize for his rendition of Dido's feelings of outrage and pain as she watched Aeneas sail off from Carthage to Italy – a creative-writing-plus-drama exercise that gave full scope to his imagination.

Then Patricius' money ran out and it was back to Thagaste to kick his heels while his father saved up to pay for the next stage in his education; which generosity, we're glad to know, was appreciated by the prospective university student. The expectation of his becoming an eminent lawyer was reward enough for his parents.

A disastrous year followed. The sixteen-year-old had suddenly nothing to do. He was utterly bored and drifted with the crowd, getting into all the kinds of trouble that a decadent, pagan society afforded. Proud of their adolescent, up-to-the-minute sophistication, they bragged to one another about their misdeeds, if not perpetrated then invented, and the pugnacious little lad who could not bear to be beaten at football was now the teenager who must keep up with the worst of them. 'I was ashamed to be surpassed in shamelessness,' he recalled. Not for him to be different!

Patricius seemed not to care and when his mother tried to remonstrate with him, warning him against the sin of adultery in particular, he shrugged off her advice – what would an old woman like her know?

One minor incident that lingered in his memory was the stripping of a pear tree. Late one night, after an evening of hanging around doing nothing in particular, one of the gang had the bright idea of robbing a neighbour's heavily-laden pear tree. It was not that they needed or wanted the fruit for they had more than enough of their own, but just for the sheer thrill of getting away with it. With a cry of 'Let's go!' they were off and in no time the tree was bare. No tempting, juicy pears these but small, unripe specimens which they fed to the pigs as they laughed and joked about the owner's reaction when he would come out next morning to behold his tree.

It was no life for an intelligent, energetic youngster. In fact it was depressing and he looked forward impatiently to setting off for the big city where he would be free to stretch his wings, where there would be life and liberty and action, lots to see and do. Thagaste was too small and dull by far.

At last in 371, at the age of seventeen, Augustine left Thagaste once more, this time travelling in the opposite direction from his previous journey. His way sloped some two hundred miles in a north-easterly direction through forests of pine and high valleys clothed in corn and dotted with olive-groves to the great city on the coast.

Chapter 5

The Cauldron that was Carthage

'And so I came to Carthage,' records Augustine, 'where a veritable cauldron of illicit loves bubbled and sputtered around me.' Certainly life in the second city of the Empire promised much excitement and he meant to make the most of his opportunities. He plunged right in.

Carthage, just outside modern Tunis, had been rebuilt on the orders of Julius Caesar and now, four centuries later, with a population of almost half a million it had all the facilities of any thriving seaport. Down by the seafront are still to be seen the extensive ruins of the Baths of Antoninus dating from the second century and over thirty years in the building. A vast complex comprising scores of rest rooms, massage parlours, saunas, pools, fountains and restaurants, it was the social centre of the city. On the rising ground inland are the remains of numerous villas of the wealthy with the theatre nearby. The usual Roman gods had a rival here – the Punic goddess Astarte, so temples abounded.

The immense amphitheatre at the foot of the hill was almost as large as the Colosseum in Rome. Here a hundred and fifty years earlier two young women, Felicitas and Perpetua, had faced the fury of wild beasts rather than acknowledge Caesar as Lord. Here too Cyprian, Bishop of Carthage, had suffered martyrdom and down by the harbour stood a chapel in his memory.

For the student fresh from Thagaste the theatre became a passion for there he found 'a mirror of my own miseries and fuel to my fire.' He especially enjoyed plays about tragic lovers, his quick empathy moving him to tears – the more the merrier! He wondered about that. How is it that one actually enjoys being made miserable over events that one would most definitely not wish to suffer oneself? 'The grief itself is what one enjoys – what madness!' he concluded. (But that was later.) The great pagan festivals also appealed to his love of drama and spectacle as did the ceremonies of the church, especially the solemnity and grandeur of the Easter vigil in the imposing basilica.

After the Edict of Milan Christians increased greatly in number and thus required larger buildings for worship. Rather than copy pagan temples they based them on the plan of the Roman basilica, the building in which the law courts were housed. They were rectangular in shape with two rows of columns parallel with the longer sides and a semi-circular projection at one of the shorter ends. There would usually be one basilica in a city but there were also smaller churches, particularly in the villages, and the bishop would be assisted by numerous lesser clergy – presbyters, deacons, acolytes and others.

At the university Augustine was studying law. He was determined to do well. Law was the gateway to advancement so when at the end of his year he came out top of his class he was, on his own admission, immensely proud and quite bedazzled at the prospect of the glittering career in the civil service that surely lay ahead.

It was about this time that news came of Patricius' death. Shortly before he died he had become a Christian. It is probable that this fact meant little to Augustine at the time for a Christian way of life was the last thing he would wish to be reminded of. Indeed, in his autobiography he passes over the event with little comment.

The financial responsibility for his

education now fell on his mother who, however, was not left to undertake it alone.

Romanianus, a wealthy citizen of Thagaste and friend of Patricius, had long taken an interest in the promising lad and, aware that his father could not afford a full education for him, had been paying part of his fees. With such backing he had better apply himself to his studies! Not that he found them demanding: all came easily to him whether logic, rhetoric, geometry, music or maths. Even Aristotle he understood on his own and was subsequently amazed to hear his professors make much ado of the difficulty of grasping the great philosopher's thought.

About this time, too, he set up house with a girl whose name is never mentioned – a sort of stop-gap wife. As a young man with ambition he had to consider carefully whom he would eventually marry. Meanwhile the present arrangement would do nicely and, besides, he liked the girl. Such relationships were common and socially acceptable. However he knew only too well that he was going against Christian principles and, although he seemed not to care, he was nevertheless saddling himself with an ever-present sense of guilt. What this girl who shared his life was like we are not told but they were together for fifteen years. In time a son, not entirely welcome at first, was born. They called him Adeodatus, 'gift of God'. It was a common enough name and may have had no special significance for the parents.

On the surface things could not be better so it was strange that his heart was restless in spite of the successes and pleasures he enjoyed. However, life was going on much as usual when suddenly his whole outlook was changed. An 'unbelievable fire' was kindled in his heart and life would never be the same again.

* * * * * * * * * * *

Augustine had been stopped in his tracks by one of his textbooks, *The Hortensius*, by the Latin philosopher, Cicero. This work, no longer extant, opened up a vista before him, firing his imagination with a vision nobler than he had known and showing up the tawdriness of his present plans and aspirations. Others might admire its language while ignoring its theme but as for him, 'It was not to sharpen my tongue that I studied it,' he recalled. 'In Greek the word "philosophy" means "the love of wisdom" and that's exactly the love with which that book set my heart ablaze.' One thing only put a brake on his enthusiasm; there was no mention of the name of Christ and nothing lacking that name, however polished, could wholly command his confidence.

Cicero, writing in the first century BC, said in effect, 'Seek wisdom; wisdom is the principal thing.' At the age of nineteen, therefore, Augustine determined to 'search after, hold on to and firmly embrace wisdom, whatever it might show itself to be.' He thought he knew where to look. 'I was on fire, my God, to fly from things of earth to Thee.... and set myself to study the holy Scriptures.' But what a disappointment! He decided that for style and elegance they could not compare with Cicero – nor were they anything like as rarefied and exalted in ideas. They spoke of ordinary men and women behaving in very ordinary, sometimes even shameful, ways.

And there precisely, for Augustine, was the crux of the matter – the problem of evil that was to keep intruding itself into his thoughts off and on, in one way or another, for years. Where did evil come from? Did it originate with man? Or the devil? But whence the devil's wickedness? There was cosmic evil and there was personal wrongdoing. What about evil impulses? Where did they come from? He soon found an answer to his questioning, or so it seemed. Like many another seeker after truth he fell in with a heretical sect, in this case the followers of Mani, born in Persia in the third century. Mani claimed to be an apostle of Jesus Christ and to have had a special revelation, the final and definitive one.

This religion, an amalgam of some aspects of Christianity and eastern religions, was more 'spiritual' than the Christianity he was used to with its (inconvenient) demands for obedience to the law of God. Moreover it had an answer to the burning question, 'Whence evil?' Manichees believed in two warring kingdoms, the Kingdom of Light and the Kingdom of Darkness. The 'higher' spiritual world is good while the 'lower' world of material things is, per se, evil. As in the world at large, so in the individual; the body is evil, the spirit is good. So those who followed this teaching, 'hearers' as they were called, saw themselves as essentially good. Any wrongdoing could be accounted for as a temporary invasion by an alien force while one's true self remained a citadel of innocence.

All very comforting. It made clear to Augustine the reason for the discrepancy between his ideals and his actual conduct – by side-stepping the issue, although he did not see that as yet. In fact for a decade he remained with the Manichees vigorously defending their position against all comers, especially Christians, and winning over many by his powers of persuasion.

Enamoured of philosophy, he now gave up all thought of becoming a lawyer. So when it was time to return to Thagaste at the end of his university course he made up his mind to teach rhetoric and literature while furthering his philosophical studies. What would Monica think of the new Augustine, the city sophisticate with his own ideas about the kind of life he would live, the profession he would follow and above all, the beliefs and ideals that would shape his life?

Chapter 6

Teaching in Thagaste

Monica did not like the new Augustine one bit. The townsfolk may well have concluded that the erstwhile hooligan had metamorphosed into the serious young professor but Monica was aghast. Three years previously he had set off full of high hopes and eager to fulfil the ambitions of his parents. Now here he was with this girl, a baby son, change of career and, worst of all, his hateful new religion. She refused to have him and his entourage under her roof. It would seem that Romanianus came to the rescue opening his door to the little family.

To orthodox Catholics Manichees were heretics, their views totally at variance with Catholic (in the sense of mainstream or orthodox) Christianity, and Monica wept over his spiritual death, as she saw it, 'more than most mothers weep over the physical death of a son, watering the earth with her tears wherever she went, and bowing her head in prayer.'

She did more; she went to see the bishop. He was good with people and she was sure that if he were to speak to the renegade he would soon come to his senses. He refused. It would be a waste of effort, he said. Augustine was in no mood to listen: the heresy was all new to him, he was full of it and glorying in his ability to confuse simple souls with his smart questions, as she herself had just told him.

'Leave him alone for a while. Keep on praying for him and he will eventually, of himself, come to realise his mistake. I myself was brought up as a Manichee, you know, and even went to the trouble of copying out some of their books but I came to see for myself, without any persuasion from anyone, how wrong their teaching was and I gave it up entirely of my own accord. It will be the same with him, you'll see.'

Monica was not convinced. More pleading, more tears. With just a hint of exasperation in his voice the good bishop kindly dismissed her.

'Go your way and may God bless you. It is not possible that the son of these tears should perish.' To Monica the words came as a voice from heaven and she took courage.

Then one night she had a dream. It wasn't an ordinary dream; she had her share of these but she also had special dreams – and she could tell the difference between them. This was a special dream. She told Augustine about it.

'I was standing on a wooden rule crying and feeling so miserable. A young man in shining robes came up to me, smiling and happy, and asked me why I was always so sad. I told him it was because of the lost, miserable condition you are in. He urged me not to give up hope but to look and see that where I was, there you were also. And when I looked, there you were standing right beside me on the same rule!'

'So, mother dear, we are going to stand side by side on the same rule. I knew it. One day you are going to come round to my way of thinking.'

'No: he didn't say, "Where he is, there you will be," but, "Where you are, there he will be." Rather different!'

Augustine was impressed – not by the dream but by his mother's cool refutation of his (deliberately?) faulty reasoning. Clearly he did not yet have the measure of Monica.

The dream had one immediate effect. Since the prodigal was eventually to return to the

Catholic faith she could open her door to him straight away and welcome him home.

So the young teacher of rhetoric passed quite a pleasant year in his home town, renewing old friendships and forging new ones. Friends were important to him all his life. Here, as in Carthage, he drew around him a group of talented and idealistic young men. Intelligent and enthusiastic they discussed all sorts of ideas – after all most of them had trained as lawyers and revelled in the cut and thrust of argument, none more so than Augustine himself especially when, as was usually the case, he emerged victorious! Under his influence many of them converted to Manicheism attracted by the austerity and high moralising tone of the sect. Among them were Romanianus and Alypius, his boyhood friend and now one of his students.

Another convert was a close friend; 'my second self,' he calls him. They had played together at school and were interested in the same things; now their friendship blossomed. Quite suddenly he fell ill. For long he lay in a fever and Augustine never left his side. As he lay unconscious, apparently at death's door with all hope of recovery gone, his relatives arranged for him to be baptised. To the surprise of all he rallied and of course heard how ill he had been, so ill that he had even been baptised. Augustine made a joke or two about that. To his utter astonishment and dismay the invalid beseeched him not to say such things if he wished them to remain friends. Augustine thought, 'When you're stronger we'll sort all that out.' Tragically the fever returned and a few days later the young man died.

Augustine was crushed. It was particularly shocking that his friend should have chosen to die in the Catholic faith. A black depression settled on him. 'He whom I loved as if he was never to die, was dead. I bore about a shattered, bleeding soul. Everything looked ghastly, even the very light' – that light which he so loved.

This death brought home to him, as his father's had not, the inevitability and the finality of death. He could no longer bear life in these familiar haunts that only served to remind him of his loss. No longer was there a frisson of anticipation as he approached the places where they used to meet but the cold reminder, 'He is not here.'

'So I fled my homeland,' he recalled.

Chapter 7

Wilderness Years in Carthage

One year after leaving it he was back in Carthage. Here for the next seven years he taught literature and the art of public speaking to the sons of the wealthy from all over Africa. Things went well for him in the city. Professionally, he was not long in making a name for himself. He won a prize in a poetry competition and had the crown placed on his head by the proconsul, Vindicianus, who thereafter took a friendly interest in him. Moreover, quite indispensable to the realisation of his ambitions, he had got to know some influential people.

In no time he was the centre of a circle of congenial friends. Alypius from Thagaste was there studying law. A new friend was Nebridius from a town near Carthage. One recurring argument he had with Augustine was over his friend's involvement with astrology. Astrology had two interwoven but distinct aspects: the first was what we would now call astronomy, a body of scientific knowledge; the other aspect was the study of the heavens for the purpose of making predictions, reading omens, making horoscopes – what we properly mean by astrology today. For many years Augustine took a serious interest in astrology and was inclined to believe that the fortune-telling of the astrologers was as valid as their science. Nebridius tried in vain to laugh him out of his addiction while the wise and much-respected Vindicianus, proconsul and doctor, warned him against the fortune-tellers and advised him to get rid of his books on the subject and stop wasting his time on such rubbish.

'But their predictions do sometimes accord with the facts,' he argued.

'That's understandable,' replied Vindicianus, 'Chance alone would guarantee as much. Now listen. As a young man I went into the subject thoroughly because that's how I meant to make my living but when I found that it was based on deceit I switched to medicine. I'm surprised that you, who are already launched on a promising career, should have anything to do with such nonsense.'

Augustine wondered. He was not going to take anyone's word for it. After all they were right about planetary orbits and equinoxes so why not about horoscopes? So he would keep his books and continue to consult the fortune-tellers from time to time – and would not give up astrology until it was made crystal-clear to him of what sort its predictions were! Above all he was bent on knowing the truth of the matter. However, the good man's arguments were lodged in his mind.

When he was about twenty-six he brought out his first book, *De Pulchro et Apto* (The Beautiful and the Fitting) of which he was immensely proud, admitting, 'If there was no one else around to praise it, I admired it myself.' He had greatly enjoyed turning over in his mind questions of aesthetics and would ask his friends, 'Do we love anything apart from what is beautiful? And what is beauty, and in what does it consist? And what is it that draws us to whatever we love?' We shall never know the outcome of their discussions for twenty years later his own copy was lost and no other survives.

For several years he continued to be an enthusiastic Manichee. But gradually doubts insinuated themselves. For one thing their astronomy was all wrong! Through his wide reading Augustine realised that there was a considerable body of accurate knowledge about the heavens: for example it was possible to predict when there would be an eclipse of the sun, and whether it would be full or partial, and how long it would last. When he compared the writings of the philosophers with Mani he found that Mani was wrong – he who claimed to be speaking by full authority of the Holy Spirit. That was rather unnerving!

Also it was a religion lacking in dynamism. He complained that there was no room for growth in it and increasingly he felt that it was glib and facile in its assumption that to know the good was to do it. He knew differently. He was only too aware of the tension between what he knew to be right and what he chose to do. However, he had to admit that the system did have its merits. 'I still held the view that it was not really I who was sinning ....' But his hold on that view was slipping.

And then one afternoon he heard a fellow-Manichee and a Christian debating and had to admit to himself that the Christian was having the better of the argument. All very disturbing and there was no one who could meet his doubts with convincing answers. None got as far as asking the questions, let alone having answers! 'But,' they said, 'wait till Faustus comes. He'll answer all your questions.'

Faustus was one of the leaders of the movement, the real expert.

Faustus did come. Augustine found him a charming, articulate man and liked him but, to his bitter disappointment, he discovered that he 'trotted out the same old arguments as the others only much better expressed.' His way with words enchanted Augustine and, even more, his honesty. When the two men had opportunity to talk together, it transpired that Faustus was, as he put it, 'quite unskilled in the liberal sciences, except in grammar and even in that he wasn't anything out of the ordinary,' and he could not even begin to grapple with the difficulties that were engaging Augustine's mind. He frankly said so and Augustine admired his modesty.

So no answers were forthcoming. He would give up expecting to make any progress in his present beliefs but would continue with them till something better should persuade him to abandon them. Interestingly, all this time it would seem that the young Adeodatus, a bright little fellow, and his mother were attached, to whatever extent, to the Catholic church.

He was disillusioned, too, with the students of Carthage, a rowdy, undisciplined lot whose behaviour would not be tolerated in any but students. They would come diving into a room, upset everything and everybody, then make off to spread mayhem elsewhere. Frustrating in the extreme. Not at all like the students in Rome by all accounts.

Some of his friends who had settled there sent word back that prospects were good: the money was better than in Africa and there were more opportunities for promotion. Why didn't he join them? Into the bargain the students were highly-motivated and well-disciplined. Serious students? He liked the sound of that! He had been long enough in Carthage. To Rome he would go.

Chapter 8

And so to Rome

Augustine had known that his mother would make a fuss and try to dissuade him from leaving Africa but his mind was made up. He was going to Rome – and, what's more, she was not coming with him!

The parting lived in his memory. 'She wept bitterly at the mention of my going and followed me to the waterfront where she clung wildly to me and would not let me go. But I deceived her as she held on, insisting that I should go home with her or she should come with me. I pretended that I wished to see a friend off and had to wait around till the wind rose and his ship could sail. So I lied to my mother – and such a mother – as I tried to get away from her.... She would not go back without me and it was all I could do to persuade her to stay the night in St. Cyprian's chapel, just a stone's throw from our ship. During the night I stole away, secretly, leaving her to her tears and her prayers .... The wind rose and filled our sails and the shore slipped from view …. She went home and I to Rome.'

What a way to go!

Why was he so determined to leave his mother behind? Was she too possessive? He hints that she was. 'She loved to have me near,' he says, 'as mothers do, but much more than most mothers.' It would seem that she had been staying, off and on, with the little family in Carthage, sometimes for prolonged periods, so perhaps he felt the need to get away from her pressure on his life – and especially from that feeling of guilt which her presence exacerbated. Did he simply need space to find himself, as it were? He was at a crossroads of a sort; perhaps it was a time for reappraisal, time for a fresh start.

After two or three days at sea (more than enough for Augustine who never liked sea-travel), the ship berthed at Ostia, the large and busy port of Rome. The provincial from Africa must at first have felt very much a stranger in a strange land in the prestigious capital of the Empire with its million and more citizens and about as many slaves. All roads did indeed lead to Rome bringing all sorts of ideas, philosophies and faiths. The newcomer made enquiries among the Manichean community and found lodging with one of them.

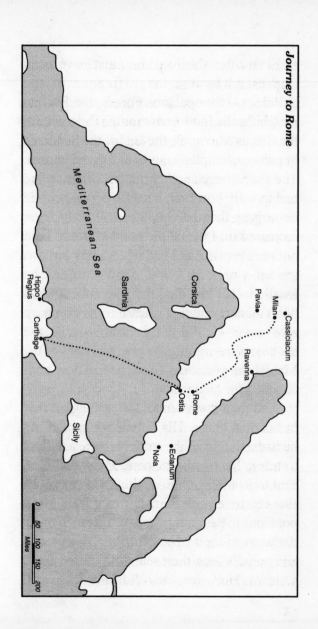

Journey to Rome

Mediterranean Sea

Hippo
Regius
Carthage
Sardinia
Corsica
Sicily
Ostia
Rome
Nola
Eclanum
Ravenna
Pavia
Milan
Cassiciacum

0 50 100 150 200
Miles

Even after Carthage he must have been impressed by the magnificence of the buildings – the spacious Forum, the Flavian Amphitheatre (now known as the Colosseum), the Circus Maximus, the Baths, the hundreds of palaces, temples, statues and grand houses. The slums were another matter! Sight-seeing had to wait, however, because no sooner had he arrived than he was taken ill. 'My fever increased till I was at the point of death. I did not seek baptism as I had when a boy but was grown worse as I was grown older,' he recalled. 'If I had died then, an unbeliever, I don't think my mother's heart would ever have recovered.' He did not die and soon he and his host were arguing the pros and cons of the Manichean system to which he had now been attached for nine years.

And then it was down to teaching, at first in his own house. His fame soon spread. As he had anticipated the students were a delight to teach. No rowdiness here. Many had been sent to Rome by their wealthy and ambitious fathers to equip themselves for leading positions in the Empire and were keen to make the most of their opportunities. They calmly and politely took their seats and settled down to learn. However, they did have their own distinctive way of doing things: when the time came to pay their fees they just as calmly and politely took themselves off in a body to another teacher. Augustine could only gnash his teeth. Students! 'This lot also my heart detested,' he confesses.

One happy find was Alypius already there practising law. A few years younger than Augustine, he belonged to a leading Thagaste family and was a relative of Romanianus. He had been a student of Augustine's in Carthage and became perhaps his closest friend. In many ways the two were contrasts. Alypius was calm, self-controlled, matter-of-fact and of an independent turn of mind. A telling incident occurred during their time together in Carthage.

He had not at first attended Augustine's classes there because of some difference that had arisen between his father and Augustine who assumed that Alypius, too, was estranged from him. Augustine for his part was dismayed to learn that his young friend was spending far too much time at the racecourse where his love of excitement and action found an outlet in viewing the dangerous sport of four-horse chariot-racing but, in the circumstances, he felt reluctant to tackle him on the subject. However, one day when Alypius had popped into his lecture-hall (as he did from time to time) Augustine was discussing a piece of writing and, to make a point, he used an illustration from the arena in which he did not mince his words in giving his opinion of those who were addicted to the games. Though he had no ulterior motive in speaking so, Alypius took it that the words were directed at him. Far from resenting this he appreciated what he understood to be his teacher's interest and concern, obtained his father's permission to enrol in the class and stopped frequenting the circus.

Now in Rome he was acquiring a reputation for an impregnable integrity. One instance involved a powerful senator who wished him to pull strings in his favour. Alypius refused. A bribe was offered. To no effect. Threats likewise. For once the senator did not get his way and Alypius became the talk of the faculty! There was one temptation, however, to which through his love of learning he nearly succumbed – to get books copied cheaply – but he thought better of it.

An interesting sidelight on his personality is provided by his attitude to the gladiatorial shows. He utterly deplored and detested the unspeakable savagery and blood-lust that were the hallmark of the arena where men fought men to the death, or were pitted against wild beasts. The gladiators, the sports stars of the day with their following of 'fans', were the professionals but besides these there was the motley crew of prisoners, slaves, miscreants and others who, however innocent, had offended the great and powerful. No barbarity was too extreme for the eyes of the connoisseurs of cruelty who flocked to the games.

One evening Alypius bumped into some friends who immediately insisted that he accompany them to the Colosseum. He desisted but laughing and excited they half-dragged him along and managed to find seats. 'I'm here but I'm not here because I'm going to keep my eyes shut and won't know a thing that's happening,' protested Alypius and he was as good as his word – till the screaming and screeching reached a climax and the crowd leapt to its feet, and he with them! No longer his own person but merely one of the pack, there he was cheering and jeering in unison with the rest, drunk with a new-found joy in bloodshed. The addictive power of violence drew him back time and time again, often dragging others with him.

He knew better than to invite his good

friend Augustine along! As for him, the creeping dissatisfaction that had overtaken him in Carthage continued to pervade his mood. He was beginning to suspect that his quest after wisdom had ended in a cul-de-sac. Manicheism he must abandon. Truth was not to be found there. Nor in the church. But then was it to be found anywhere? Was he chasing a will-o'-the-wisp? Probably the Academics were right, he concluded. These philosophers maintained that it was impossible to find truth – or so he understood them to say. So perhaps the best course was to be content with not knowing. To a certain extent this cleared his mind, gave him breathing-space, but he was not one who could long be happy in such a state. He craved certainty if it could be attained. Meantime, for want of anything better, he would keep up his connection with the Manichees.

So when the Prefect of Rome, Symmachus, let it be known that a professor of literature was required in Milan and that travelling expenses would be paid, he applied for the post. With Symmachus' commendation and through the good offices of his Manichean friends he was successful. He had been in Rome for one year only and was glad to leave.

Chapter 9

Milan

It was autumn 384 when the twenty-nine-year-old Augustine arrived in Milan, three hundred miles north of Rome. Situated in the broad and fertile plain of Lombardy and some thirty miles south of the snow-capped Alps, it was the busy meeting point of all the roads in northern Italy. The imperial court was there presided over by the boy Emperor, Valentinian, and his mother.

Milan was a lively, cultural centre and the new professor of language and literature found it exhilarating. He was quite taken up at first with the novelty and interest of it all. His post was an important one. One of his duties was to act as an official spokesman for the court and he was also expected to give speeches on public occasions. That should bring him into the limelight! Milan was the place to be for an upwardly-mobile young man.

Upwardly mobile socially, perhaps; inwardly at a standstill. Manicheism had proved fruitless; the church likewise. He was adrift on a sea of doubt.

Almost immediately he fell under the spell of Ambrose, Bishop of Milan, whom he later dubbed 'my pole-star.' About eleven years older than Augustine, he belonged to a noble Roman family. His early years had been spent in Trèves where he was born in 339 but when his father died the family moved to Rome where he qualified as a lawyer. After practising with great success at the bar he was appointed provincial governor of northern Italy with his residence in Milan. There in 374 on the death of Bishop Auxentius he was acclaimed bishop by sudden and clamorous consent. The story goes that a row had broken out among the differing factions as to who should succeed to the office and as Ambrose, in his capacity as governor, was trying to restore order a child's voice rang out, 'Ambrosius Episcopus!' Immediately the crowd joined in; 'Ambrose for bishop! Ambrose for bishop!' Thus was he compelled into office. This had become quite an accepted way of choosing a bishop.

The city soon felt the impact of his lively preaching and godly life. Soon after arriving in Milan Augustine called on him to pay his respects and retained a glowing memory of how 'as a father' the good bishop received him. There developed a mutual respect and affection. And how happy he must be, thought Augustine, to have everyone think so highly of him. (Shades of his own preoccupation!) He went to hear him preach, not in pursuit of truth, a forlorn hope as he would then have thought, but to see if he deserved his reputation as a speaker, for he had the craftsman's appreciation of another's skill. Nevertheless he had to admit, 'Though I was not interested in what he had to say, but only in how he said it, yet alongside his way of expressing himself, which I liked, the teaching too, which I didn't care about, made its way into my mind for I did not know how to keep them apart.'

Here were sermons that were both polished and learned. Ambrose was at home in all the classical learning of his day as well as in the Scriptures and Christian literature. Augustine heard him pronounce on philosophers past and present, including the Hebrew philosophers of the Old Testament and to his considerable surprise he found the criticism levelled by the Manichees against the latter completely demolished.

Moreover, and crucially, Ambrose introduced him to a whole new way of looking at the Scriptures. A favourite quotation of his was 'The letter killeth, the spirit maketh alive.' He treated many of the Old and New Testament stories as allegories, emphasising that it was their hidden meaning that mattered – an altogether more satisfactory way of looking at them, thought Augustine. In fact as he attended the services every Lord's Day he discovered that many of his objections to the Catholic faith were due to misunderstandings on his part.

Still, difficulties remained – mostly the questions that have engaged the minds of men down the ages. The problem of the freedom of the will was one. Another was the idea of God. He had always believed that God is, and that He rules over His universe 'even to the fluttering of the leaves on the trees'. Now to his surprise and joy he discovered that the Church did not teach that God was a human shape as he had thought it did, but how to conceive of Him still eluded him for he could only think in terms of the physical. To read an account of his mental contortions as he grappled with this problem evokes a sympathetic smile.

And always nagging away in the background that puzzle, 'How is it that there is evil in a world made by a good God? Where, and how, did it originate? Or is there no such thing? Why then fear it if it does not exist? And why is it allowed to continue?' and so on and so on. His difficulties were compounded by his imagining evil as some sort of physical mass creeping about the earth with malign intent. Nor were these questions merely academic; they were intensely personal. ' I was feverishly looking for the origin of evil. What torments came from the agitation of my heart, what groans, my God…. and when in silence I sought earnestly, the unspoken contritions of my soul were great cries for your mercy.'

But when he thought of approaching the renowned teacher with some of the questions that were perplexing him he could not get near him surrounded as he always seemed to be by needy people whom he gladly helped. Or else he would be reading 'but not aloud,' he recalled. 'His eyes scanned the page while voice and tongue were still and, after sitting a while in silence we would slip away unwilling to distract him from the work in which he was so absorbed.' One way or another the moment never seemed opportune.

Gradually, however, his mind was won over to the extent that Christianity now seemed intellectually respectable. The Scriptures made sense. He had a new respect for them. But were they true? He was not convinced that the church was teaching the truth but at least it was not teaching what he had thought it did.

Ambrose was one formative influence. Plato was another. The Greek philosopher was enjoying something of a comeback. His reading of the Neo-Platonists, particularly Plotinus and Porphyry, had a profound and lasting effect on Augustine. They pointed to an ultimate reality above and beyond the here-and-now of this world; they, in fact, clarified his thinking about the spiritual and the material – a major development which both freed him from his fruitless attempts to envisage God and gave him an integrated world-view. 'I came to see that though things above are better than the things of earth yet the totality of the creation is better than the higher things alone.'

There was, however, a glaring lack in Plato, 'that noble philosopher', as there had been in Cicero all those ten years ago – no mention of Christ, no word about salvation or how to deal with sin, no 'Come unto me all ye that labour.' And if anyone was labouring, he was, heartsick from hope deferred. Ten long years and here he was stuck in exactly the same morass! The more he delved into philosophy the more he realised that these brilliant Greek thinkers, these seekers-after-wisdom, for all their insight and for all their imagination, were yet like men who could see the land of far distances but could not find the way to it. In fact he confided to Alypius and Nebridius that he would willingly plump for Epicurus with his philosophy of 'Eat, drink and be merry for tomorrow we die' – if only he were convinced that death was not followed by judgement.

But he was convinced otherwise and was going to keep on with his quest. His great fear was that he might once more be deceived. This time he wanted to get down to rock-bottom reality. As it often happens that one who has suffered at the hands of a bad doctor finds himself reluctant to entrust himself to a good one, so this time he wanted to be sure – as convinced about spiritual matters as he was that seven and three make ten. Otherwise he would not commit himself.

Then he reflected that there were myriad matters in life that he took on trust – who his parents were, when he was born, reports about places he had never visited, events in the past – purely on the evidence of others. The suspicion was forming in his mind that after all his mother might be right. So he resolved, 'For the time being I will plant my feet firmly on those steps on which as a child I was set by my parents, till such time as the clear truth may be found,' – but not all that firmly for he adds that he was still drifting up and down, despairing of ever finding truth.

Round and round his thoughts churned in search of the ineluctable he-knew-not-what that would give meaning to life, thoughts such as, 'Tomorrow I shall find it. The Academics are wrong. Searching must bear fruit. But where to begin? Ambrose has no time. And I've no time for reading either. Anyway what books? And how to find the time? I'm teaching all morning. The rest of the day? There are influential friends to keep up with. And lectures to prepare. And everyone needs a break – especially from anxious thoughts. Life is wretched and death can come at any time. What if it should come suddenly, what then? Perhaps I should turn my back on the affairs of this world and devote myself entirely to finding God and true happiness? But hold on! I can't do that! Getting on in the world has its place. Indeed, what more would a man wish for? I've lots of friends in high places and with a little help from them I might even be given a post as governor. And, who knows, a nice wife might happen along (rich preferably to help with expenses) – There now, that would do me nicely!'

Such was the turmoil in Augustine's mind when on to the scene came Monica.

Chapter 10

Enter Monica

It was late spring when Monica arrived in Milan, some six months after Augustine. Over sea and land she came, she who feared the sea, braving a storm that had the very sailors afraid for their lives. Like Paul on the same wind-whipped Mediterranean she assured all on board that they would arrive safely. She knew; God had told her so in a vision. And so it turned out, and here she was in Milan and it was her son who was in peril.

They hadn't seen each other for almost two years. As they got talking he had news for her, he said – he had given up his Manichean ideas. He was not a Christian; but neither was he a Manichee. Monica took the news calmly, perhaps too calmly for his liking, but she now knew that she could not dragoon him into the faith. So far so good but only half-way. 'I am trusting in Christ, that before I depart this life I'll see you a Christian yet,' she promised.

She began to attend Ambrose's preaching, loving him 'as an angel of God' because she knew that it was through him that Augustine had been brought to such wavering faith as he then had. She humbly learned from him herself, too. In Africa she had been in the habit of offering gifts of bread and wine and little cakes at the shrines dedicated to saints but here in Milan she found that the practice was not encouraged by the bishop – and, to Augustine's astonishment she meekly acquiesced. The bishop for his part congratulated Augustine on having such a humble, teachable and generous mother, 'not knowing what a son she had in me!' he comments.

The following February she had an opportunity to demonstrate her loyalty and gratitude to him. Justina, the Emperor's mother favoured the Arian heresy. She ordered Ambrose to hand over his church for use by the Arians. He refused. There was quite a stir in the city. A sit-in was organised and Monica was there with the praying congregation, ready to die with their bishop. To lift their hearts, for the first time psalms were sung in the church as was the custom in the churches of the East. The danger passed but the habit of singing the psalms continued. By June Ambrose had faced out the court and was ready to enter the new basilica which he had built. It was dedicated to the Holy Apostles and became known as the Basilica Ambrosiana.

Meanwhile Monica had taken charge at home. It was time Augustine thought of a suitable marriage, she insisted and he agreed. If he was to make his mark in the world he must acquire a wife of some social standing. Enquiries were made while Monica prayed that God would guide them by means of a dream but, for all her praying, no clear assurance was given. However, their united efforts were crowned with success and he became engaged to a young heiress two years under marriageable age. He liked her and was willing to wait.

Telling his mistress was not easy. They had been together for fifteen years and were genuinely fond of each other. However, she would have to go. Had he been an eminent, high-born person, the status of his wife might not have mattered too much but he was still struggling to make his way in the world so ....

The parting was painful to both. She was 'torn from my side as a hindrance to my marriage,' is how he remembered it years later; she returned to Africa leaving her twelve-year-old son behind and vowing that, for her part, she was finished with men. As for him, he loved her dearly and his heart 'which had been one with hers was crushed and bleeding.' Within a few months he had replaced her – and despised himself for it – while the pain which had felt like an amputation gave way to a persistent, dull ache. Fifteen years could not be shrugged off lightly.

His friends were a lifeline. He confessed that he could not live without them, talking and laughing together, doing one another favours, discussing books, sometimes jolly, sometimes serious, on occasion arguing but without malice, more often agreeing, teaching and learning from one another, missing those who were away and welcoming them with open arms on their return.

Alypius was there pursuing his legal career, more to please his parents than himself. Nebridius had come to Milan just to be with Augustine. As the son of a wealthy pagan family he had no need to earn his living and so was free to enjoy the luxury of a life devoted to quiet and undisturbed study. Intelligent and full of common sense he was not one to be fobbed off with easy answers. A hard question demanded hard thought and there must be no shirking! His mother had no intention of following him to foreign shores, opting rather to remain in their grand estate in the country. Augustine had one piece of good news for him. He had finally been forced to admit to himself that astrology was all a delusion and so was freed from its tyranny. Another shackle gone!

This group of friends discussed endlessly and frankly the big – and little – questions relating to the meaning of life. About ten of them decided to withdraw from the frantic busy-ness of life and live together in a community of peaceful endeavour. They would pool their resources and take it in turns, a year at a time, to be responsible for the material needs of the group thus leaving the others free to pursue their quest of truth.

Romanianus, who had come to court on business, was enthusiastic – which was handy for he was by far the wealthiest. They discussed the details at length and had everything neatly sewn up except for one small matter. Some of them were married and when all had been talked over thoroughly their wives were consulted. What did they think of the plan? Not much, it seems, so 'that scheme which had been so well put together came to pieces in our hands and we reverted to sighs and groans and continued to walk the broad and beaten ways of the world.' Still, it remained a beckoning dream.

Although still ambitious Augustine was becoming increasingly ambivalent about his career. He was successful all right but what was he achieving, he wondered: training young men to talk cleverly – if, indeed, such skills could be taught – not in the interests of justice (that would be something) but simply so that they could get their clients off; delivering flattering speeches at the court of the Emperor, speeches which everyone knew to be full of lies – how futile! No wonder he was jaded!

He even got to envying a beggar he came across in the street, the worse for drink but merry with it. 'See how happy he is – at the cost of a few pence,' he remarked to Alypius, 'while I chase, with endless fear and anxiety, a happiness that always eludes me.'

Chapter 11

A Severe Mercy

Into this state of uncertainty and inner turmoil came a new influence. Under Ambrose's teaching Augustine had come to accept the Bible. His views of its teachings had changed and he was now reading Paul's letters and there found the truths he had admired in Plotinus – and many more. It was one thing, he realised, to see from a wooded mountain-top the homeland of peace and try in vain to reach it through pathless ways; another thing entirely, to keep on the path that leads surely to it, safe in the care of the heavenly guide.

His ideas about God had also changed. 'I wondered that I now loved Thee and not a phantom of my imagination in place of Thee; and yet I did not press on to enjoy my God though I was drawn by Thy beauty .... I did not doubt that there was One to whom I could cling, but I was not yet the person who could cling.' Sometimes he experienced a longing, like a precious memory, a whiff as it were, of a food which he was not yet able to taste.

But as he became more and more convinced of the truth of Christianity he became ever more uncomfortable. He saw only too clearly the implications for living. 'The way, the Saviour of the world, pleased me well but I could not find it in my heart to follow it through the strait gate.' In acute agitation and deep oppression of spirit he felt himself being pulled in two directions. 'I had now found the goodly pearl and, selling all that I had, I ought to have bought it but I hesitated.' What was holding him back? He confesses, 'I was still bent on acquiring riches, fame and a wife!' and he thought that all these had to be renounced if he became a Christian (and perhaps in his case that was so).

He decided to talk things over with Simplicianus, a friend of Ambrose and a Christian. The old man listened and congratulated Augustine on reading Plato for, of all the philosophers, he came nearest to Christianity; as a matter of fact he had once met a Platonist who said that the words, 'In the beginning was the Word ... and the Word was God' should be written in letters of gold across the heavens. He then proceeded to speak of his friend, the great Victorinus, whose translation of Plato Augustine had been reading. Late professor of rhetoric in Rome, his statue now stood in the Roman Forum. A highly-educated pagan he had given his life to the study of philosophy and used his oratorical gifts to stir up the people to the praise of the gods. He also studied the Scriptures and other Christian writings and one day confided to Simplicianus that he had become a Christian. Simplicianus' response was, 'I'll believe it when I see you in the church of Christ.'

'So it's walls that make a Christian?' laughed Victorinus. Each time he brought up the subject he received the same reply – and made the same retort!

Eventually his fear of offending his pagan friends was overcome by his fear of offending Christ and so it came about that one day he approached Simplicianus with the request, 'Let us go to church; I wish to be received as a Christian.'

He was enrolled as a catechumen and shortly afterwards applied for baptism 'to the wonderment of Rome and the joy of the Church,' reminisced Simplicianus.

In Rome the custom was that those making a profession of faith did so in a set form of words which they memorised and then recited from a raised platform before the congregation. As a well-known public official who might find it embarrassing to acknowledge a turnaround in his views, Victorinus was given the option of making his confession in private but he would have none of it, and as he appeared before the people a glad murmur ran through the crowd, 'Victorinus, Victorinus!' followed by a sudden hush as they waited for his words. With freedom and confidence he made profession of the true faith and the listeners drew him to their hearts.

As he listened to Simplicianus Augustine's heart burned within him with a longing to do as Victorinus had done. But still he hesitated and the weeks dragged by. He was in a kind of torpor. 'Now I was sure of the truth. Yet, still in bondage to earth, I refused to fight under Thy banner and feared as much to be freed from all my cumbersome baggage as I ought to have feared being hindered by it.... All I could manage by way of response was a sleepy "Soon .... in a little while .... I won't be long" but my "Soon" stretched on and on.' It was what he called 'the chain of habit' that paralysed him. 'My will was held by the enemy who thus made a chain that bound me.

A wilfully perverse act gives rise to the desire to repeat it; when desire is satisfied a habit is formed; when habit is not resisted a kind of compulsion takes hold. By these close-knit links I was held fast.'

The story of the unlikely convert, Victorinus, wordsmith and lover of philosophy like himself (and, he knew, more famous than he would ever be!) stayed with him. A little later in that summer of 386 the story of two obscure men was to bring him face to face, inescapably, with the central truth about himself.

He had rented a house with a small garden and sharing it with him, besides Monica and Adeodatus, were Nebridius and Alypius and possibly some other friends. One afternoon towards the end of August when Augustine and Alypius were alone, they received an unexpected visit from a fellow-African, Ponticianus, a highly-placed official in the Emperor's court and a Christian. As they chatted their visitor picked up a book that lay on the games-table nearby and to his surprise found it was the *Letters of Paul* – not exactly what he expected Augustine to be reading. In the course of conversation he began to speak at some length about Anthony of whom his listeners confessed they had never heard.

Ponticianus was astonished. They'd never heard of Anthony? The Egyptian monk esteemed in all the churches? Nor of the many monasteries inspired by him? But they must surely have heard of the monastery just outside the walls of the very city they were now in? Ambrose often visited it. That reminded him of one afternoon in Trèves when he, Ponticianus, and three friends had gone for a walk in the gardens near the city walls. They divided off into pairs.

The other two happened upon a cottage where lived a community of monks. They entered and one of them picked up a copy of the *Life of Anthony* and was soon engrossed in reading. Suddenly he burst out, 'Tell me, what are we aiming at in life? What do we hope to gain by all our straining and striving? At best the Emperor's favour!'

As he read on it became clear that a struggle was going on in his heart. He spoke again. He had, he said, renounced his worldly ambitions and would henceforth, from that very moment, devote his life to the service of God and he begged his friend not to oppose him if he would not join him. To which the other replied that he, too, would engage in a service so glorious.

Ponticianus and his companion duly caught up with them at the cottage to be told by their friends that they were leaving the Emperor's service forthwith and 'with hearts set on Heaven' were remaining with the monks. Nor was that the end of the story. The two were engaged to be married and when their fiancées heard what had happened they followed their example and entered a convent.

Such then was the story that Ponticianus told while Augustine listened, at first enthralled and then shaken to the foundation of his being. He remembered it vividly. 'While he was speaking, Lord, Thou wast turning me round towards myself, taking me from behind my back where I was hiding so as not to see myself. Thou didst set me before my face and made me look at myself.... I stood aghast, but there was no way of escape from myself....'

Vignettes from the past flashed before him; the beginning of his quest with his reading of Cicero all those twelve years ago (twelve years!); his intermittent and half-hearted prayer, 'Give me chastity – but not yet'; the wilderness years in Manicheism; subsequent wanderings...

But Ponticianus had finished his business and took his leave. 'I turned to Alypius, my face mirroring the agitation of my mind. "What's the matter with us? Did you hear that? These two, with none of our education, have taken heaven by storm while we, for all our learning, still wallow in flesh and blood." He looked at me in astonishment but said nothing. My voice sounded strange even to myself .... Driven by the tumult in my breast I fled into the garden where no one would interrupt the fierce struggle I was having with myself till it should finally be resolved.'

Alypius followed. Together they sat at the far end of the garden while Augustine beat his forehead, tore at his hair and locked his fingers round his knees, as 'soul-sick and tormented I twisted and turned in the chain that bound me.' One voice within was insinuating, 'From now on you will not be allowed this or that for ever. Do you think you will be able to live without them?' Another asked: 'What makes you think you will have to stand in your own strength? Cast yourself on God. He will receive you and heal you.' So back and forth raged the controversy within while the secrets dredged up from the depths of his soul piled up in a heap before his mind.

Overcome by a storm of weeping, and choking out some few words to Alypius, he stumbled off to find a spot where he could be alone and, throwing himself down under a fig-tree, he gave full vent to his feelings. Acutely aware that he was held fast by his sins he kept crying, 'O Lord how long? How long? Wilt Thou be angry for ever? How long shall I go on saying, "tomorrow"? Always tomorrow! Why not now? Why not be finished with my ugly sins now?'

And then, clear as a bell, from over the garden wall came the sound of a child's voice chanting over and over again,

'*Tolle, lege; tolle, lege;*'
'Take it up and read it,
'Take it up and read it.'

Augustine's attention was caught. He listened.

'*Tolle lege; tolle, lege.*'

Was it a boy or a girl? He could not tell. Were the words part of a game? He could not recollect ever having heard them before. Perhaps the words were a message from God? He remembered what he had just been told about Anthony, how he had walked into church as the Gospel was being read and had taken to himself, as a personal command from God the words, 'Go, sell all that you have .... and come, follow me.'

'*Tolle, lege ....*'

He would obey the command; he would open the book and read the first passage his eyes should fall upon. He knew which book, the *Letters of Paul*, which he had left on the seat beside Alypius. Hurrying back to where Alypius still sat with the book beside him he seized it, opened it and in silence read the words that leapt from the page; '.... Not in rioting and drunkenness, not in chambering and wantonness, not in strife and envying. But put ye on the Lord Jesus Christ, and make not provision for the flesh to fulfil the lusts thereof.'

Marking the place he closed the book and put it down. 'There was no need to read further,' he recounts, 'for in an instant, as I came to the end of that sentence, it was as if a steady light shone into my heart dispelling all the darkness and doubt.' A new life had begun.

Now calm and composed he told Alypius all that had happened. He in turn revealed what had been taking place in his heart and asked to see what his friend had read. He then read on to the following words; 'Him that is weak in the faith receive.'

'That's me,' he said and hope warmed his heart. Straight away, naturally, they went to find Monica. As they related the whole story she broke into jubilant praise of God who had answered her tearful prayers above all her asking or thinking. Her dream of years long gone had come true. Now at last her wandering son stood where she stood on the rule of faith and her tears were tears of joy.

Chapter 12

Time Out

The most that Monica had dared hope for was that her wayward son would become a good Christian, follow an honourable calling (with fame and fortune thrown in?) and settle down with a suitable wife; and perhaps she could look forward to having more grandchildren around her.

Augustine had other ideas. For one thing he was resolved to give up his career. This was partly to do with the asceticism that he mistakenly thought was a mark of the more devoted Christian and typically there were to be no half measures with him. In any case he had already had thoughts about a change of direction. For some time he had been troubled with a pain in his chest and had breathing difficulties, perhaps stress-related. Added to which his voice had become strained so that he could not speak for any length of time – he, a professor of rhetoric! All in all he had been feeling that perhaps his days of full-time teaching were numbered. The autumn holidays were only three weeks away so he would remain in his post till then.

So the idea of a philosophical retreat surfaced again. He and Alypius were beginners in a new school and had much to learn. A quiet interlude devoted to reading and thinking seemed called for. As for grandchildren, Monica would have to be content with those she already had. At that time Augustine's (and probably Monica's) ideal of the Christian life was the single life. So Augustine's fiancée was told that the wedding was off.

What to do next? Verecundus, a citizen of Milan and teacher of literature, for whom Nebridius had done some lecturing, came to the rescue. Although his wife was a Christian he himself was not and his friends' conversion left him feeling rather out of things. Nevertheless he generously offered them his country villa at Cassiciacum and Augustine and his household took up residence there in late September.

Cassiciacum was probably on Lake Como, near the foothills of the Alps. With Augustine, besides his brother, Navigius, and Alypius, 'the brother of my heart', were two of his students – Romanianus' son, Licentius, a bright and bouncy lad who wrote poetry and

Trygetius (who was to become a Roman senator and die a Christian). These two were about sixteen years of age. His son, Adeodatus, with two cousins, Rusticus and Lastidianus, were also in the party and presiding over all, needless to say, was Monica.

There was time for reading, conversation and structured discussion. The substance of their discussions is found in four books he wrote, basically philosophy imbued with Christianity. Each was encouraged to think for himself and Augustine's flair for teaching had full scope. But it was not a rigorous regime. There was ample leisure for the pursuit of individual interests and for just 'sitting thinking'. And for letter-writing.

Augustine wrote to Ambrose asking his advice as to what he should read and was recommended the prophecy of Isaiah but he found it too difficult and studied instead the Gospels and the Psalms. He especially liked Psalm 4. It described his experience. 'Hear me when I call, O God of my righteousness: when I was in distress Thou hast enlarged me... Thou hast put gladness in my heart ... I will both lay me down in peace and sleep: for Thou, LORD, only makest me dwell in safety.'

The soul-searching of these days finds

expression in the *Soliloquies* in which he debates with himself in an effort, as he says, 'to find out my real self.' He wrote it himself; there was no one present taking down notes; there was no discussion with the others. Here he was probing his own being, finding out where he stood, pondering the implications for the future. It begins with a prayer:

Oh God, from whom to turn away is to fall;
To whom to turn is to rise again;
From whom to depart is to die;
To whom to return is to revive;
In whom to dwell is to live;
Whom no man loses unless deceived,
Whom no man seeks unless encouraged,
Whom no man finds unless made pure;
To abandon whom is to perish,
To reach out to whom is to love,
To see whom is true possession,
By whom death is swallowed up in victory....
Draw near, I pray, and show me Thy mercy.

This work, which meant so much to him, is a self-portrait in which he probes into his own psyche and attempts to think through how he relates to God. 'After Thee am I groping ... No one seeking Thee aright has failed to find Thee; and every one seeks Thee aright whom Thou dost cause so to seek Thee. Teach me how to come to Thee; I have nothing but the will; I know nothing but that the fleeting and failing should be spurned, the certain and eternal sought. This I do, Father, for this is all I know; but how to make my way to Thee I know not. Do Thou make it plain, equip me for the journey! If they who take refuge in Thee find Thee by faith, give me faith! If by virtue, give me virtue! If by knowledge, give me knowledge .... I desire to know God and the soul – nothing more.'

'To know God and the soul' is as good a summing-up as any of what would be the lifelong activity of his lively, enquiring mind. His interest embraced the twofold aspects of truth, both as reality and as a truth to be lived. He never ceased asking, 'Why? What is meant by ...?' He would delve into such questions as the nature of time: 'What is time? If no one asks me, I know: if I wish to explain it to someone who asks, I don't know,' – but he has a good try, all the same!

Book Two of the *Soliloquies* begins with a dialogue between himself and his reason:

Augustine: Let us set about this second book.
Reason: Let us do so at once.
Augustine: And let us believe that God will be with us!

Reason:	Let us truly believe this if that, indeed, be within our power.
Augustine:	Our power is Himself.
Reason:	Pray then as briefly and concisely as you can.
Augustine:	God, always the same, let me know myself, let me know Thee! The prayer is made.
Reason:	You, who desire to know yourself, do you know that you are?
Augustine:	I do.
Reason:	How do you know this?
Augustine:	I do not know ....

Being Augustine he did not leave the question there! Anticipating Descartes' '*Cogito ergo sum*' by a millennium and more he came to the conviction, 'I am most certain that I am, and I know and delight in this. With regard to these truths I am not at all afraid of the arguments of the Academics who say, "What if you are deceived?" For if I am deceived, I am.'

As he convalesced in the peace and beauty of the countryside Augustine felt a calm of mind and spirit such as he had never known. He experienced the truth of his own saying; 'Thou hast made us for Thyself and our hearts are restless till they find their rest in Thee.' The tranquillity of their surroundings, the limpid autumn days under Italian skies, the clear air filled with bird-song and the distant snow-capped hills melting into limpid skies matched the serenity of his heart. It was sunshine without and sunshine within. 'These holy days,' as he recalled them, not even a bout of toothache could spoil. Together they prayed and the pain vanished.

Monica was in her element mothering and managing them all to her heart's content, never too busy to put her oar in when the discussion warranted it. Augustine's thirty-second birthday was celebrated with a simple dinner followed by a discussion which lasted three days and ended up in the book, *The Happy Life*. At one point he put forward for consideration the question, 'Is the man happy who obtains what he desires?'

Monica didn't hesitate.

'If what he desires is good and he obtains it, he is happy. But if he wishes for what is evil, even if he gets it he is miserable.'

Augustine was proud of her.

'Mother,' he beamed, 'you have attained the summit of philosophy! Though you lack the language in which he elaborates it, you have expressed perfectly the thought of Cicero in his *Hortensius*, a book he wrote in the praise and defence of philosophy.' Those halcyon days he was to remember to the end of his life.

Autumn melted into winter and then in early March the little party returned to Milan where Augustine, together with Alypius and Adeodatus, joined the class for candidates for baptism. Ambrose himself took the six week course of instruction.

On Easter Eve, 24 April 387, they made their way to the great basilica to join in the psalm-singing, readings and prayers of the worshippers. Monica was there in her place; this was the night for which she had wept and longed and prayed. At the appointed time the three with the other *competentes* made their way to the octagonal baptistery adjoining the basilica. (The remains of the baptistery may still be seen though the basilica has disappeared.) Leading down to the central pool were three concentric rows of steps, the lower of which were laid in colourful mosaics of fish and other sea-creatures.

Here the bishop presided. Each candidate in turn stepped down into the pool of running water.

He was asked,

'Do you believe in God, the Father, the Almighty?'

'I do believe.'

'Do you believe in the Lord Jesus Christ?'

'I do believe.'

'Do you believe in the Holy Spirit?'

'I do believe.'

He was then baptised by Ambrose. The white-robed neophytes then made their way in procession to the basilica, ablaze with candlelight, where the packed congregation waited. All joined in worship and the singing of the great throng filled the building. The symbolism of the psalm might have been chosen for this night:

O send thy light forth and thy truth:
  let them be guides to me:
And bring me to thine holy hill,
  even where thy dwellings be.
Then will I to God's altar go,
  to God my chiefest joy:
Yea, God, my God, thy name to praise
  my harp I will employ.

'All anxiety over our past life left us,' Augustine remembered. 'I couldn't get enough in those days of meditating with delight on the deep things of Thy plan of salvation. The singing of psalms and hymns in church moved me to tears. The music flowed into my ears and the truth penetrated my heart. So deeply was I affected that tears ran down my face. They were tears of happiness.'

The household had by this time been augmented by the arrival of Evodius, a recent convert, who belonged to Thagaste and who had lately resigned from the civil service. He had held an important post in Rome and was, moreover, a friend of Ambrose. He went on to become the Bishop of Uzalis. The little group of whole-hearted Christians deliberated much as to their future course and came to the conclusion that they could best serve God by serving their fellow-countrymen in Africa. To Thagaste they would return and there set up their community.

So off they set on the long journey to Rome and its sea-port where they expected to board ship for Carthage. To Ostia, the great, bustling port at the mouth of the Tiber they came. Here they were brought to a standstill.

Chapter 13

Ostia

No ships were sailing from Ostia. Rivalry between Emperor Theodosius and Maximus had resulted in a blockade of the harbours of Rome by the General. There was nothing for it but to stay put.

Archeologists have seen to it that we have a fair picture of fourth century Ostia. It had by that time seen better days but still behind the little houses crowding the harbour stood the mansions of the nobles in spacious grounds and, most splendid of all, the truly magnificent palace of the wealthy Anicii family who, like many of the nobility, were Christians. It is likely that Augustine and his party found hospitality with one of these families for it was in a spacious house, secluded from the din of men by a courtyard and garden, that they waited out the embargo.

That house was to be forever etched in Augustine's memory. One day he and his mother stood alone at a window overlooking the garden. As they talked together they got to wondering what heaven would be like. Augustine later tried to describe what happened but language could not match the experience; words and images tumble over one another, a medley of Christian concepts and Platonic thought-forms. Their imaginings ranged from the beauties of earth and the awesome vastness of space to the mysterious powers of the human mind and spirit, while they speculated as to what the everlasting now might be like, the thoughts of one a catalyst to the other's. Together, he remembered, they 'attained to one moment of understanding' and 'in swift thought touched on eternal wisdom.... If life could for ever be like that one moment of understanding, wouldn't that be entering the joy of the Master?'

As they thought of the things 'which eye hath not seen, nor ear heard, neither have they entered into the heart of man....' Monica suddenly turned and said, 'My son, as far as I am concerned, I have no further delight in anything in this life. Why I am here or what I have still to do here I do not know, now that all I hoped for in this world has been realised. For one thing only I lived, to see you a catholic Christian before I should die. God has more than answered my prayers; not only are you a

Christian, but you are turning your back on the world to devote your life and service entirely to Him. What more have I to live for?'

Five days later Monica lay gravely ill with a fever and soon slipped into unconsciousness. As the quiet, precious hours passed her little family kept watch, each with his own thoughts. Suddenly, as Navigius and Augustine stood by her bed, she opened her eyes and asked, 'Where was I?' adding after some minutes, 'Here, in this place, you must bury your mother.'

'Oh mother,' said Navigius, 'we hope you will not die in a foreign land. You always said you wished to be buried in your own country.'

Which was indeed true. She had often expressed the wish that no matter how far she might travel, she might return to rest beside her husband so that as they had been united in life so they might be united in death. She had even made practical arrangements for that eventuality. But she was no longer concerned about the matter.

'Listen to him!' she said. 'No; lay this body of mine anywhere at all: don't let that worry you in the least. There's only one thing I would ask of you; remember me at the Lord's altar, wherever you may be.'

She spoke little after this, growing daily weaker and after nine days' illness she died. She was fifty-six.

'I closed her eyes and a great sorrow filled my heart,' Augustine recalled. 'My eyes filled with tears but with a great effort I restrained them.'

The young Adeodatus could not contain his grief and wept aloud but was soon hushed by the others. It was not right, they said, to lament and grieve as those who have no hope for she was not unhappy in her death nor, truth to tell, was she altogether dead.

Instead of weeping they sang. Evodius began, 'I will sing of mercy and judgement:' and the others joined in. Soon the house was filling up with friends and the word of praise rang out:

Unto Thee, O LORD, will I sing.
I will behave myself wisely
    in a perfect way.
O when wilt Thou come unto me?
I will walk within my house
    with a perfect heart.

Augustine was, perhaps misguidedly, determined not to show his feelings. 'When the body was taken out for burial I went and returned without tears; even when prayers were offered as her body lay by the side of the grave I did not weep.... They must all have thought I felt no sorrow, but I knew what I was suppressing in my heart. All day I was weighed down by sorrow, a double sorrow for I grieved on account of my grief, reproving myself for grieving so deeply something that I had known must, in the nature of things, come to pass one day.'

Perhaps if he went to the soothing waters of the baths he would feel better; after all, didn't the Greek derivation of the word signify 'that which banishes sorrow?' So to the baths he went and, not surprisingly, came back not one whit better. He went to bed and slept. When he awoke the words of a hymn by Ambrose came to him:

> Creator, God most high,
> Who rules the earth and sky,
> Who clothes the day with light
> And gifts with sleep the night,
> That refreshed we may
> Be strong for working day
> Our minds from care set free,
> Heart's sorrows healed by Thee.

And then, at last, he gave way to the tears he had been holding back and, he recalled, 'I wept my heart out for a mother dead and gone from my sight, who for years had wept over me that I might live in Thy sight....' And he remembered his mother's words as she lay dying and they comforted him; she had said more than once that he had been a good and dutiful son, and never had she heard him speak a harsh or reproachful word to her.

She had wanted no great fuss at her funeral nor any imposing memorial. Some friends told him how, one day shortly before she became ill, she had been talking with them and had said how little this world had to offer in comparison with the next, to which death would be the gateway. They said, 'But would you not be afraid to leave your body here, so far from your own town?'

'No,' she replied. 'Nowhere is far from God. He will know where to find me at the Resurrection and raise me to life again.'

* * * * * * * * * * * * *

In 1945 two boys playing football beside the Church of St. Auria in Ostia began to dig a hole for a goalpost and unearthed a piece of marble. From the inscription it appeared that it was a fragment of Monica's tombstone.

Chapter 14

Home to Africa

Since it looked as if it might be some time before anything moved in the bay, the band of friends made for Rome, there to wait out the blockade, and were to remain there for just over a year. There they heard that Verecundus, who had so generously lent them his mansion at Cassiciacum, had died but not before becoming a Christian. Augustine was confident that God was now repaying his kindness with 'the pleasure of Thy Paradise forever green'.

Towards the end of 388 Augustine and his African friends were back in Ostia and leaving Italian shores – in Augustine's case for ever. What memories must have flooded back as the ship pulled out from shore!

The momentous years in Italy were telescoping behind him as the sails filled and the land receded and finally slipped from view: Italy, where in a sense life had begun anew for him. The two day voyage gave opportunity for reflection on the past and speculation as to the future. Gazing out on the ever-changing swell, 'trying on its many colours, now varied shades of green, now purple, now blue' as he describes it, it would be strange if his thoughts had not gone back to the outward journey when he had slipped away from his mother despite her tears; now he was leaving her body in the land where her prayers had been answered and her weeping for ever stilled.

The coastline of Africa hove into view and soon they would be landing in Carthage. He was coming home; yet before him lay 'fresh fields and pastures new' for he himself was in many ways a new man. So in late autumn 388 after an absence of five years he found himself back on African soil. After a brief stay in the home of the good Innocentius they continued their journey to Thagaste where they settled on Augustine's little family estate – Alypius, Evodius, Severus, young Adeodatus and others. They were known as *Servi Dei*, Servants of God, a recognition that they were dedicated Christians living in obedience to God, but as laymen, not as an ordained order.

Any resemblance to Cassiciacum was superficial. Life in the small community in which he had grown up could never be an oasis of peace. True he intended to devote himself to prayer, writing and study – of the Scriptures principally, having deliberately left most of his books behind in Italy. But teenage tearaway, crusading Manichee or *Servus Dei*, Augustine could never be less than totally committed. Almost immediately he was engaged in a running battle with the local Manichees who were strong in Thagaste as in Africa generally. He addressed the wider Manichee audience in his book *On True Religion* which he dedicated to Romanianus. In it he points out that the Christian doctrine of the Fall explains the presence of evil in the world as their teachings never could. Eventually he came to the conclusion that evil is a negative, a lack rather as darkness is an absence of light. 'Evil has no nature; but the loss of good, that is evil.'

Nebridius was not with them. He was still with his mother on their country estate near Carthage and was now a Christian as were his whole household through his influence. The two friends kept up a lively correspondence. Nebridius wrote:

Is it true, my beloved Augustine, that you are expending your strength and patience on the affairs of your fellow-citizens, and that the freedom from distraction which you so keenly looked forward to is still denied you? Who, I should like to know, are the men who thus take advantage of your good nature and trespass on your time? I'm sure they do not know what it is you most love and long for. Is there no one among your friends there who will tell them what it is that captivates your heart? Won't Romanianus or Lucianus do this? Then let them listen to me! I'll tell them that you love God above all and that your heart's desire is to be His servant and to live close to Him.

I wish I could persuade you to come to my home in the country and rest with me here – even if I should be denounced as a robber by those countrymen of yours, whom you love only too well and by whom you are too warmly loved in return!

Interestingly, Nebridius frequently asked Augustine what his thoughts about heaven were. Augustine for his part begged his friend to join them in Thagaste but Nebridius declined. Indeed it soon appeared that he could not do so; he was ill and one day news came that Nebridius, 'my sweet friend', the true-hearted and genuine seeker after truth, had died. Augustine comforted himself with the thought that he was now endlessly happy and would still remember them for if God did, wouldn't he who was in communion with God remember them also?

These years in Thagaste were marked by another death. Adeodatus died suddenly at the age of seventeen, his father's son in intelligence with a bright, enquiring mind. A taste of their discussions at Cassiciacum appears in *Of the Master*, a dialogue between the two in which we are assured that the ideas attributed to the boy are his own. Augustine observed with a kind of awe the abilities with which God had endowed him. His parents had brought him up in the Christian faith and his father could remember him without anxiety. 'I fear for nothing in his childhood or in his youth nor, indeed, do I have cause for any misgivings whatsoever regarding him.'

Life had changed radically from the cosy picture he once had in mind. There was now the emptiness and loneliness of grief. The two years in Thagaste were a hiatus, a sort of recouping and reorientating period, an interval between the old ideal of philosophy and retreat and a new life of involvement in the affairs of the Catholic church – but the extent of that involvement he little anticipated.

Chapter 15

The Monastery in the Garden

The last thing Augustine wanted was to be a bishop, so he was careful to avoid any city which he knew to have a vacancy lest he be hijacked.

However, he had no fear on that score when he decided to visit Hippo about seventy miles away on the coast for it already had a bishop. He was going to see a friend whom he hoped to win for God and, besides, he had been keeping an eye out for a place in which to set up a monastery and one never knew .... So, wearing the short black cloak or birrus that denoted the servant of God off he set one fine spring morning on the road that climbed the ridge to the north and then sloped down through wooded country and lush plain to the ancient seaport.

In the event his friend hummed and hawed and procrastinated while Augustine explored the city and attended services in the basilica. The bishop, Valerius, was an old man and moreover a Greek with no great facility in Latin and none at all in the Punic dialect of the country folk. He was feeling his years and had impressed on his flock the necessity of appointing an assistant. They lost no time. While standing all unawares among the congregation Augustine was grabbed and with the customary clamour propelled forward to the bishop's throne. There and then he was ordained presbyter and some wondered if the tears he shed were because he had not been ordained bishop!

So it was that Augustine came to Hippo Regius at the age of thirty-six, there to spend the rest of his life. Occupying the site of the modern city of Annaba it was one of the most important cities in Africa. It was built on two low hills round a fine bay on the western edge of the Seybouse valley with the towering headland of the Djebel Edough as backdrop. As a pre-Roman town, already a thousand years old, it was built in a more haphazard fashion than the typical Roman town, which it had been for a mere two hundred years. The large forum and temple looked down on the town from the top of the higher hill. The theatre at its foot held five thousand. Between it and the harbour were the public baths and the basilica with its adjacent baptistery and, beyond them overlooking the harbour, the stately villas of the wealthy with their beautiful, mosaic floors. As well as a thriving seaport Hippo (meaning 'shelter') was the centre of a rich agricultural trade with all the associated comings and goings of people and ideas.

Augustine lost no time in setting up his monastery near the basilica. To his considerable delight it was surrounded by a garden. He wrote, 'Is there any place where one is in closer touch with the nature of things than when one is busy sowing seeds, taking cuttings, transplanting bushes or grafting slips? You feel as if you could question the life force in each root and bud as to what it can, and what it cannot do,' adding typically, 'and why.' The consideration of the power in one single seed filled him with awe. He once said that the miracle of turning water into wine at the marriage in Cana is not marvellous to those who know that it was God's doing, for He does the same every year in the vineyards – rain from the clouds is changed into wine in the grape but we do not wonder at it because it happens every year.

Such confidence had Valerius in his assistant that straight away he invited him to preach, a privilege normally reserved for the bishop. Thus began a remarkable ministry that was to make its influence felt not only throughout Africa but throughout the whole Christian church down to the present day.

He was uniquely fitted for this position in Hippo: he had come to his present convictions after long struggle, had seen consistent Christian living at close quarters in the life of his mother, had lived in sophisticated cities and a small town and found it easy to mix with all sorts of people, from the intelligentsia to the simple country folk. Even the fact that he had been a Manichee stood him in good stead! And, not least, he never forgot what he had been.

His fame spread. Valerius was delighted; the Lord had heard the prayers he had so often sent up to Him for 'such a man as this'. In 395, at his suggestion, Augustine was appointed his bishop coadjutor and on Valerius' death the following year he succeeded him as bishop. He wrote, 'I do not intend to live in the empty enjoyment of ecclesiastical privilege but mean to keep ever in mind the fact that I must give an account of the sheep committed to me.'

Unlike many of the bishops he took his work seriously. And there was work in plenty to be done – visiting the sick, expounding the creed to his fellow bishops and debating with his old friend, Fortunatus, still a Manichee, (and routing him so completely that he fled the town!). He was often asked to arbitrate in disputes – where he was much happier to decide between strangers than between friends; of the two strangers one would become a friend while of the two friends one would become an enemy! In addition to which, there were the legal affairs of his people to be seen to as this formed an inevitable part of a bishop's work; indeed, many bishops saw it as their main task. Then there was the ongoing work of evangelising the villages which had, till his arrival, been left to the Donatist church. He complained that he could never get enough men to go out and preach to the country folk in their own dialects and attributed their many misunderstandings about Christianity to the lack of the Scriptures in their own language.

The monastery was not to be a Cassiciacum with self-improvement as its focus. Its raison d'être was to serve the church and the community so it was more like a theological college from which graduated a steady stream of young men to fill sees throughout Numidia and farther afield in Africa, doubtless with Augustine's stamp upon them and always sorely missed by him when they left. Alypius, soon to become Bishop of Thagaste, stayed there for a time as did Evodius.

Life in the monastery was well-regulated but not rigid. Time was given to prayer and study but also each was expected to earn his living by 'a common workman's lowly toil' as he put it. He had no time for 'hypocrites dressed up as monks, roaming the countryside, sent nowhere, settled nowhere, standing nowhere, sitting nowhere, some carting about the limbs of martyrs (if you were to believe them) and all of them begging for money.' He was wholeheartedly of the mind that 'if a man will not work neither should he eat.'

The Rule of Augustine, drawn up about ten years later, is marked by practical common sense and a warm humanity. By that time asceticism as such had no place in his scheme of things. To those who insisted on walking barefoot in even the coldest weather, for instance, (as had Alypius at one time in Italy) he made a plea for tolerance; 'I admire your courage; won't you put up with my weakness?' And (snug in sandals and socks!) he reminded them that such practices had no special merit in themselves.

All things were held in common. Meals

were shared. The main meal of the day was served in late afternoon. Dishes were of wood, pottery or marble and the spoons of silver. The food was adequate rather than plentiful. Guests (and there were many for he was the most hospitable of men) and those in need of extra nourishment might be served meat but otherwise it was rarely on the menu. There was a fixed allowance of wine for each. The food, however, was of only secondary importance; reading and conversation were the main consideration. Malicious gossip was out. As a reminder, round the table was carved in Latin the rubric:

> He who would slander an absent friend
> May not at this table as guest attend.

Clothes were supplied from a common fund. In general Augustine refused to accept gifts lest he be accused of enriching himself though here, too, he knew when to waive a rule. On one occasion he was given a tunic which had been made by a nun for her brother who, like Augustine, was evidently short and slight. He died suddenly and she thought it would fit their friend. He wrote:

I have accepted the gift woven by your own clever, devoted fingers because I should not wish to hurt you when you are in special need of sympathy. You assure me that it will give you no small comfort if I wear the tunic that was originally intended for your brother, that holy servant of God. Now that he has left the land of the dying and has no further use for things that perish, I have not only accepted it but I have started to wear it. Be of good heart – but above all seek after consolations far greater and higher than mine. You have, I know, much cause for grief. You can no longer gaze, as you used to do, upon that brother who so dearly loved you; no longer watch him engage in the duties of the altar; no longer hear from his lips the words of frank praise with which, in that brotherly way of his, he used to pay tribute to his sister's sanctity ....

Your brother, my dear child is alive in soul though dead in body. "Shall he that sleeps rise again no more?" The God who has already received his spirit will give him back his body which He took not to destroy but to restore. There is thus no reason for prolonged sorrow but rather every reason for everlasting joy for his visible appearance, his greeting and conversation, the very inflection of his voice, as familiar to your ear as his face was to your eye – even these are not lost to you for ever....

These are the promises of the One who has

so fulfilled His other promises that we may well believe that these also will be fulfilled. Let your faith dwell on these thoughts because your hope shall not be confounded even though for a while it may be difficult to exercise your love. Turn them over and over in your mind; they contain solid and very real consolation. If the simple fact of my wearing (because he could not) the garment you made for your brother eases your hurt, how much more comforting should be the realisation that he for whom it was prepared and who, by the time it was finished, no longer had need of a perishable garment, shall be clothed with incorruption and immortality!

Convents offered an alternative way of life for girls who were often married off at an early age. It was not their vows as such, Augustine pointed out, that commended them but their love to Christ; indeed, some of the martyrs had been married women – like the noble Perpetua who was the mother of a young baby when she met her death in the arena. Augustine's widowed sister, another Perpetua, was prioress for many years of a convent near the monastery in Hippo and Navigius' daughters lived there also for a time.

As ever he kept up a voluminous correspondence with friends and acquaintances, including Jerome in Bethlehem who was making a fresh translation of the Scriptures into Latin. They did not always see eye to eye for in spite of a reciprocal respect the two had the knack of getting on each other's nerves. However it was not all contention. In 394 Alypius visited Bethlehem and Augustine, pleased to have firsthand news, subsequently wrote:

> When he saw you there I was seeing you myself with his eyes, for all who know us may say of us that we are two in body only not in mind, so great is the union of heart, so intimate the friendship between us – though in merit we are not alike for in that respect he far outshines me.

But if you wanted to know Augustine really well you had to hear him preach. So said his biographer, Possidius, and he should know for he lived with him in the monastery for about six years before becoming Bishop of Calama. In the Basilica of Peace, with a capacity of almost a thousand, he would sit on the raised cathedra with his listeners standing before him, attentive but by no means passive. As likely as not there would be shorthand-writers taking down his words and, not unlike the hustings there could be comments of agreement, interested questions, the occasional heckler – an interaction between preacher and people. He did not have a powerful voice and had to take constant care that he did not strain it. Sometimes he had to appeal to their sympathy; 'Yesterday the crowd stood packed together into the furthermost corners and people were not very quiet which made it difficult for our voice, which is not strong enough to be heard by all unless there is absolute silence.'

The subject-matter of his preaching was the Word of God, as it was the final court of appeal in all matters of doctrine. And then there was the business of communicating that knowledge to his congregation. Though trained in rhetoric where style was all, in his preaching (which was in Latin) Augustine went for simplicity and directness, but it was the simplicity of mastery – always just the right word, the memorable illustration, the resonating allusion, for it was his burning desire to make his people understand and respond.

He followed Ambrose's allegorical style of interpreting the Scriptures. Here he is preaching on the Samaritan woman in John's Gospel; 'Jesus told her, "Call your husband." Husband typifies the mind, the understanding. She had five husbands, signifying the five senses of the body. But why are they called husbands? Because they are lawful and right, made indeed by God and are the gift of God to the soul.'

Listen to him on the miracle of the feeding of the five thousand. 'To run it over briefly: by the five loaves are to be understood the five books of Moses; and, quite rightly, they are not wheaten but barley loaves because they belong to the Old Testament and you know that with barley it is hard work to get at the kernel for it is covered by a tough husk. That's the way with the letter of the Old Testament, but if we get at its kernel it feeds and satisfies us.' On Moses striking the rock in the wilderness he comments: 'The Rock was smitten twice with a rod; the double smiting signified the two wooden beams of the cross.'

Numbers were significant. 'It was the tenth hour. That number signifies the law because the law was given in ten commandments.' 'The man at the pool of Bethesda waited thirty-eight years. Now we must carefully explain how this number refers more to weakness than to health.'

The typology was not arbitrary; though some of the analogies may seem far-fetched, and the argumentation sometimes convoluted, the whole was consonant with the general drift of Scripture, and in an age when people had to rely on their memory the method doubtless had the incidental merit of being a useful aide mémoire, while the occasional wordiness that can obtrude in the written form might even be an advantage when addressing a congregation open to interruption.

He engaged their mind. 'You know the question before us; now seek out the answer. But to make the solution desirable let us repeat the theme. The point that concerns us is this; why does the evangelist say, "For Jesus himself testified that a prophet has no honour in his own country"? Thus spurred on let us go back to the preceding words....'

He appealed to the mind but also to the heart and the imagination and also, one might say, to the subconscious. They responded to him and he in turn to them, quick to notice signs of flagging and ready with a change of mood or style, something to engage them fully again. He could paint a picture in a few words: 'You see a bent old man, ploughed all over with wrinkles, leaning on his stick and scarcely able to move. You hear he is a good man and you immediately love him and embrace him.' ' The man who rises at night to dig through his neighbour's wall, how much better for him to be tossing on his bed with fever.' Quoting the psalmist's 'Hence from me, wicked men' he adds, 'It's as if he was swatting them away like flies dancing before his eyes.' Again, 'Jesus says, "No man can come to me, except the Father which hath sent me draw him." Hold out a green twig to a sheep and you draw it. Show nuts to a child and he is attracted – drawn by love, drawn by a cord of the heart.'

He identified with his listeners. 'When you hear the Lord say, "He who hears my words and does them not" (now let each one of us fear and beware)....'

He began from where they were and led them on. 'When you hear the Lord say, "Where I am there also shall my servant be," do not think merely of good bishops and clergymen. But let you yourselves also in your own way serve Christ by good lives, by giving alms, by preaching His name and doctrine in your own way.' Every father, he reminded them, may discharge the debt of love he owes his family by showing kindness and exercising discipline and so in his own home be a kind of bishop and servant of Christ.

The distinctive note of his preaching was what came to be known as the theology of grace. Briefly, he taught that all are sinners because Adam, as the representative of the human race, had chosen the way of disobedience. We just do not have it in us to come up to God's standards and are consequently in a hopeless state as far as self-help is concerned. So much for the bad news.

The good news, the gospel, is that God has come to the rescue. Help is available – and it is free. 'Since we did not deserve to have our sins forgiven but yet have received this great benefit, it is called grace. What is grace? It is what is freely given. What is meant by "freely given"? Given as opposed to paid. If it was due, it would be a case of wages being paid, not grace bestowed.' So if God demanded holiness he must give it – or faith or anything whatsoever. Let Him command what He will but He must give it.

To his congregation he urged, 'Let them that hear understand. Do not understand in order to believe, but believe in order to understand. *Credo ut intellegam.*' And above all he insisted that right belief must issue in right practice. 'You may seek after honours and not obtain them, may labour for riches and remain poor, may pursue pleasures yet have many sorrows. But our God, of His supreme goodness, says, "Who ever sought Me and found Me not or desired Me and failed to obtain Me? I am with him who seeks Me, and he who seeks Me is sure of My love." Behold, the way to Him is neither long nor difficult.'

But he held that a preacher was not a mere dispenser of information. His words must take wings. Even then he must not rely on his preaching; there must be a teacher within or his words would be useless.

His verdict on his own efforts? In a letter he wrote, 'With me it is almost always the case that my preaching displeases me. I long for something better; my powers of expression fail to match what I see with my mind's eye and I am grieved when I find that my words do not adequately express what is in my heart.'

Chapter 16

Bishop of Hippo Regius

More and more Augustine took a leading part in the African church. His good friend Aurelius, Bishop of Carthage, agreed with him that there was much room for reform. They tackled the growing abuse of the traffic in relics and also the custom of meeting at the graves of martyrs. Originating as pious acts of remembrance (as observed by Monica, for instance) these had deteriorated more often than not into little more than occasions of revelry and excess. The practice of deferring baptism till just before death he opposed and through time the practice of infant baptism was established.

Reforms within and controversies without – that was the story of the church in Africa. From Augustine's cathedral could be heard the hearty singing ('more like the roaring of lions,' he exaggerated) of the Donatist congregation along the road. The Donatists were strong in Africa, and between the two groups there was continual strife. The Donatist movement arose after the ferocious persecution instigated by Emperor Diocletian in 303. Churches were destroyed and Christians were ordered to hand over their books, especially the Scriptures, to the burning. Thousands stood firm, even to death, but many capitulated in the face of torture. The persecution lasted off and on till the Peace of Constantine in 313 when Christianity became the favoured religion of the Empire. With peace came recrimination. Donatus became the leader of those who held that the *traditores* (literally the 'handers-over', the traitors) should not be readmitted to the fellowship of the church unless they were rebaptised. They maintained that ministers who had denied the faith had forfeited their right to administer the sacraments and should not be reinstated. The movement grew rapidly and soon its followers in Numidia outnumbered the Catholics.

Donatus became the bishop of their church in Carthage. When asked to arbitrate between the rival claims of Caecilian, the Catholic bishop, and Donatus to be the true bishop in that city the Emperor pronounced in favour of Caecilian. Donatus grew to resent the state's interference. 'What has the Emperor to do with the church?' he famously demanded.

Such were the origins of the dispute but long years had passed and circumstances had changed. At bottom it was a disagreement about the nature of the church and the validity of the sacraments. The Donatists stood for a church that was, in a sense (and to put it rather bluntly), above reproach while Augustine saw the church as a field in which must be allowed to grow both wheat and tares till harvest-time. Otherwise they taught the same doctrines and there was no question of the Donatists being regarded as heretics. Of course other matters came in and muddied the waters.

The two groups resorted to coercion in their different ways. An extreme wing of Donatism took to looting and terrorism. Possidius, by this time Bishop of Calama, was attacked by a band of these Circumcellions (or camp-followers) who set his home on fire and beat him up. Augustine, too, was a target and on one occasion owed his escape from their attentions to the mishap of losing his way and taking the wrong road.

Finally the Emperor Honorius intervened. The bishops of both churches were called to a conference. On 18 May, 411 two hundred and eighty-four Donatist bishops converged on Carthage followed by a like number of

Catholic bishops. The opening session was scheduled for the 1st of June with the fair-minded and devout Flavius Marcellinus in the chair (metaphorically speaking, for the Donatist bishops remained standing, and as a layman, Marcellinus felt he must also stand). Alypius, one of the official spokesmen for the orthodox church, could not resist musing aloud on the pity of it that other towns did not enjoy the peace and unity that prevailed in his Thagaste. Possidius had his outraged say. In spite of their best efforts, however, by the end of the second session the Donatists, under the leadership of Petilian of Cirta, looked all set for a heady triumph. On the 8th came Augustine's turn to speak. He stepped forward and, quite extempore, dealt point for point with the Donatist argument and won a resounding victory for the Catholics – at least that's what it felt like when, in the early hours of the next day, Marcellinus announced the verdict; the Donatists had no case. The state then intervened and tried to do by force what persuasion had failed to do – drive the Donatists into the mainstream church. For Augustine it was a hollow victory. Though at first he felt that force was justified on the grounds that the unpalatable medicine was for their own good, the prospect of the church being inundated by reluctant converts from Donatism ultimately lost its appeal and he came to distrust the alliance between church and state. To add to his disillusionment the faithful Catholic, Marcellinus, got on the wrong side of the authorities; on 13th September 413 he was arrested, taken to a public park and beheaded.

All such matters of faith and doctrine had to be hammered out in conference and Augustine took an increasingly leading part. So though never fond of travelling he was, oftener than he could have wished, to be found clip-clopping on horseback here and there as he attended councils of the church, socialising with his fellow-bishops en route to Carthage or inland to other towns (though never a mention of Thagaste, which may mean nothing at all) with everywhere a sharp eye for the peculiarities of human behaviour – the gambler venting his frustration on his dice, the fond owner painstakingly teaching his parrot to tell a joke, the patient shrieking at the surgeon's approach. And wherever he went he was chosen to preach so that, he lamented, he was prevented from following James' advice to be swift to hear, slow to speak!

These controversies generated some of his writings, the subject-matter of which was generally theology-with-a-purpose; that is to say they dealt with particular issues, were driven by contemporary events, explored questions that people were asking at that moment.

On the surface this would not appear to be the case with the book that is perhaps his best-known work, the *Confessions*, written around 397 during the early years of his bishopric, but even it is closely connected with his developing theology. It is in a sense a real-life example of how God acts in grace – and had acted in Augustine's own life.

The book is shot through with quotations from the Scriptures which he so loved. It is the story of an inward journey, of the windings and twistings on the tortuous path to his present position. The unlikely saint paints a picture of himself, warts and all. He writes with unflinching honesty before God, to whom it is addressed throughout, as he searches out the hidden motives of his heart. He was aware that people might have an unrealistically high estimation of him (as happened with bishops) and he wanted none of it – he was still afraid of his old tendency to covet the praise of men.

People wanted to know about him – so he would tell them. Describing his teenage years he homes in on what looks like a comparatively trivial boyhood ploy – the robbing of a pear tree. He puzzled over that pear tree. It was the very pointlessness of the deed that intrigued him. It provoked the same old questions as do acts of vandalism everywhere: why did he do it? what did he get out of it? what was the point? As he wrestled with the problem he had to conclude that he did it just for the sheer love of doing what was wrong. That's what was so disturbing about it; that was the really telling thing – it was simply sinning for sinning's sake. That showed something about the core of his being. To sin for some gain or other is bad enough – but to steal just because you want to do wrong! He hated to think about it.

That's the kind of person he was, a sinner in need of forgiveness as were they all. But God had saved him. He confesses, 'Thou didst cry and call aloud and burst through my deafness; Thou didst flash and shine and didst shatter my blindness; Thou didst waft sweet fragrances, I breathed them in and I pant for Thee; I tasted, and hunger and thirst for Thee; Thou hast touched me and I burn for Thy peace.'

The strong impression emerges that while he may have begun by writing for others he was soon writing also for himself. After telling where he had come from he goes on to explore where he is now, for people were clamouring to know that too. Not that he had arrived. Like Paul he could say, 'Not as if I had already attained but I press on…..' and for this, too, he is dependent on God. He tries to assess what progress he has made in the life of grace – as far as he can understand himself, that is, for much of what he is is hidden from himself. 'I am a problem to myself,' he says. 'There is in me a lamentable darkness by which my potentialities are hidden from myself so that when my mind enquires into itself it is wary of trusting its own report.... My whole hope is in Thy mercy. Lord, give what Thou dost command and command what Thou wilt.'

The question of how we know God leads him on to a detailed analysis of memory which he judged quite awesome in its power and complexity. He was fascinated by psychology: 'Men go abroad to admire mountain peaks, the mighty billows of the sea, the broad sweep of rivers, the circle of the ocean and the procession of the stars, and yet they do not marvel at themselves.' It is, he said, God who has given man his mind and he never ceased probing into its workings. Many thought-provoking insights, sometimes in throwaway remarks, are scattered throughout his sermons, books and letters. Writing to a friend he describes how imagination is dependent on perception; 'No one can have a conception of a colour which he has never seen, or a sound which he has never heard, or a flavour which he has never tasted or a scent which he has never smelled.... However it is possible, by subtracting from and adding to images which the senses have introduced into the mind, to imagine something which itself was never perceived by any of the senses.... When we were boys, born and brought up in an inland district, we could form some idea of the sea from seeing water in a cup: but in no way could we imagine the flavour of strawberries or cherries before we tasted them in Italy.' There are references, among others, to the subconscious, the association of ideas, the psychology of motivation.

It is his willingness to dig deep into the well-springs of motivation that make the *Confessions* such a compelling book, perennially up-to-date. He wrote it, he said, for the encouragement and stirring up of the weak and for the delight of the good that they, his companions of the way, might rejoice with him – and surely his aim has been realised. As an old man he could look back and say, 'The thirteen books of my *Confessions* praise the just and good God in all my evil and all my good ways, and stir up towards Him the mind and feelings of men: for myself, that's the effect they had on me when I wrote them, and they still move me, when I read them now, as they moved me when I first wrote them. What others may think is their business: I know that many of the brethren have enjoyed them, and still do.'

One of those who was impressed (and irritated beyond measure) by the *Confessions* was a British monk a few years younger than Augustine. They had arrived in Rome about the same time but did not meet. Unlike Augustine, Pelagius had stayed on in the capital. Personable and upright, and a professing Christian, he was appalled by the low moral state of many in the church, their materialistic outlook, their love of wealth and luxury. He put this down to their beliefs and set himself to stir them up to better things. What particularly annoyed him in Augustine's work was his recurring plea 'Give what You command and command what You will,' and he set himself to attack the thinking behind it.

Essentially Pelagius was saying that human beings were not so very bad; all that talk about sin was exaggerated; people are born innocent and what they need is encouragement to follow Christ's example. If you keep telling them they are sinners what can you expect but that they will live up to your assessment of them? In a letter to a nun, Demetrias, he wrote, 'Whenever I have to speak of laying down rules for the conduct of the holy life I always point out first of all how human nature works and show what it is capable of....' And his estimate of that was perfection; it was simply a matter of choosing the good and refusing the evil. 'Moreover,' he stated, 'since perfection is possible, it is obligatory.' Daunting words! There is a superficial plausibility about his views especially when life is flowing along smoothly. Of course, it all depends on what one means by perfection. His views, which came to be known as the British heresy, were gaining wide acceptance and Augustine knew that, attractive at first sight though they were, they were totally at variance with the heart of the Christian message.

In reply to Pelagius' book *Nature*,

Augustine wrote, *Nature and Grace*, *Grace and Freewill* and much more. He acknowledged his opponent's integrity and good intentions (and admired the clarity of his writing) but maintained that his diagnosis of mankind's ills was all wrong. Pelagius, he felt, had an inadequate view of the complexity of human nature; the human condition was too desperate for man to tackle on his own. In contrast to Pelagius' do-it-yourself prescription he maintained that salvation must come from outside man. All, young and old alike, are in need of it. As for the apparent innocence of infants, that springs more from the feebleness of their limbs than from the intention of their mind – one look at a baby, arms and legs flailing and face screwed up in rage or jealousy, should dispel all doubt! Nor did his arguments rest on his insights into human nature, profound though they were, but on what he found plainly stated in the Scriptures. A favourite quotation was 'Work out your own salvation with fear and trembling for it is God who worketh in you both to will and to do of His good pleasure.'

The note of realism in Augustine's teaching together with the expectancy of help in daily living, resulted in an optimism that was lacking in his opponent's with its 'you're-on-your-own' philosophy; it freed men in all walks of life to be enterprising, to be forward-looking, to attempt great things for God. His thinking he summed up in the aphorism, 'Without God we cannot; without us God will not.'

Ultimately, in 417, Pelagius was excommunicated but his views live on. They were taken up by Julian of Eclanum for one, the brilliant son of Bishop Memorus, a friend of Augustine. At thirty years of age he became Bishop of Eclanum in Apulia and proclaimed Pelagian views while miscalling Augustine and Alypius. A long and bitter war of words ensued.

One work that was written in response to a specific situation is his masterpiece, *The City of God*, which took him all of thirteen years to write though the event that occasioned it condensed into one earth-shaking night the creeping malaise of half a century.

Chapter 17

The City of God

Throughout the fourth century Christianity had been gaining in respectability (too much so, thought Augustine; it meant the church was flooded with nominal Christians). By the beginning of the new century the public and private practice of paganism had been outlawed: idols and statues had been destroyed; temples were closed and some had even been turned into Christian churches. It sounds like news to make a bishop happy. Augustine's letters, however, convey a sense of impending doom. The church was becoming more worldly and corrupt. The grandeur that was Rome was diminishing. Everywhere were to be seen the signs of decay and declension, in the neglected buildings as in the fabric of society. For centuries the Empire had been harried by Germanic tribes to the north but now Huns, Vandals, Visigoths and others were causing trouble.

Then the unthinkable happened. On the night of 24 August, 410 Alaric the Goth in a surprise attack breached the walls of Rome and for three days the invaders burned and ravaged the city which had stood impregnable for eight centuries. Mansions and temples were ransacked and carts were piled high with the plunder. Pelagius was there at the time and remembered it in a letter to his friend, Demetrias:

> Rome, the mistress of the world, shivered, crushed with fear at the sound of the blaring trumpets and the howling of the Goths. Where, then, was the nobility? Where were the fixed and distinct social classes? All were mingled together and shaken with fear; every home had its grief and an all-pervading terror gripped us. Slave and noble were one. The same spectre of death stalked before us all.

The psychological impact was immense, far outweighing the material damage. The 'eternal city' symbolised stability, justice and security; it appeared as the very bedrock of civilisation itself, a necessary bulwark against chaos. Now men's hearts failed them as they looked into an uncertain and doom-laden future. When the news reached Bethlehem Jerome mourned, 'The city which has taken the whole world is itself taken!' and wondered if anywhere could now be safe.

144

Augustine wrote, 'Tidings of terror are reaching us. There has been massacre, fire, looting, murder and torture.' Good pastor that he was his first concern was to encourage his flock. Let them look around, he urged. The olive groves were laden with fruit. To yield their oil the olives must be pressed. In the same way the world was being pressed that good might come of it.

'You are surprised that the world is losing its grip, that the world is growing old? Think of a man: he is born, he grows up, he becomes old. Old age has its many troubles: coughing, shaking, failing eyesight, anxiety, tiredness. A man grows old: he is full of complaints. The world is old: it is full of pressing tribulations .... Do not hold on to the old man, the world; do not refuse to regain your youth in Christ, who says to you, "The world is passing away, the world is losing its grip, the world is short of breath. Do not fear. Thy youth shall be renewed as the eagle's." '

Refugees, many of them belonging to the aristocracy, came pouring into Africa and Hippo got its share, both Christian and pagan. Among the former was Anicia Faltonia Proba, widow of the wealthiest man in the Empire. He had once addressed the young Ambrose when a catechumen with the somewhat prophetic words, 'Act not as a magistrate but as a bishop!' Proba had supported a small community of nuns who did not belong to any ecclesiastical order but lived with her in her splendid palace in Rome. This kind of arrangement was comparatively common. With her now were other members of the family, including her young grand-niece, Demetrias. When, three years later, the fourteen-year-old Demetrias renounced an auspicious marriage in favour of becoming a nun (though living at home with others of like mind) the news caused quite a sensation. Jerome wrote offering advice. Pelagius wrote a very long letter. Augustine was quite delighted to have had first-hand information and wrote to her mother, Juliana:

You have filled my heart with joy at an announcement that was very gratifying to one who holds you in such great affection, and very welcome since it was sent so promptly. The news that your daughter has consecrated her life to God by a vow of virginity is being noised abroad in all places where your family is known – in other words, everywhere. But you forestalled the swiftness of the reports and told me in your letter so that I was in possession of

146

certain and reliable facts and could rejoice in the accomplished deed, blessed and noteworthy as it is, without having to question the truth of rumours.

Another arrival was Volusianus, an able and cultured member of an old Roman family. He was the leader of a group of educated young men who articulated what they saw as the need of the hour – a return to the good old days when the pagan gods guaranteed the glory of the Empire: 'When we sacrificed to our gods Rome flourished; now when people everywhere sacrifice to your God, and our sacrifices are forbidden, see what is happening to Rome!' They must go back to the religion and the culture that had made Rome great in the first place. Christianity seemed to these Romans (as to the Greeks before them) as mere foolishness compared to the wisdom of the great philosophers of their past. It was time, they argued persuasively, to rescue these philosophies and to rebuild their civilisation.

Augustine knew that the intellectual and philosophical challenge had to be met. So, somewhat reluctantly, he set to work on what was to become his *magnum opus*, an apologia of Christianity against paganism in no less than twenty-two books, begun in 413 and finally completed in 426. Its immediate purpose was to help people to view the sack of Rome in a wider context, to put it in perspective, but it proved an absorbing task – not a task, rather an interest that captured his imagination and warmed his heart as he developed a Christian philosophy of history from the creation of the world till the end of time.

The City of God is an exploration of two cities, the city of God and the city of this world. Their citizens constitute two groups of the human race – those who live according to God's will and those whose lives are lived without reference to God. The two groups intermingle and overlap in this world but the fundamental difference between them will affect their ultimate destiny. So though earthly kingdoms and empires – even the Roman Empire – may crumble and crash, the kingdom of God will remain and continue to the second coming of Christ at the end of time. Following the analogy used in Scripture, he elaborates the theme of the people of God as strangers on this earth, in the world but not of it, with their citizenship in heaven. They look for a city and, as Isaiah promised, 'the ransomed of the LORD shall return, and come to Sion with songs and everlasting joy upon their heads:

they shall obtain joy and gladness, and sorrow and sighing shall flee away.'

That does not mean that Augustine despised this world so rich with the Creator's gifts. Alongside the miseries and troubles of life there are innumerable joys. He loved colour and beauty (we remember that his first book had been on aesthetics) and above all light, 'the very queen of colours.' His boyhood roamings in a landscape golden with sun in summer, dazzling in winter, had given him a love of light, such that he felt quite depressed if deprived of it suddenly or for any length of time. He speaks of 'the extraordinary brilliance and shimmering of the light in sun and moon and stars, and in the dappled shades of a glade; the colour and scents of flowers; the sheer diversity and abundance of chirruping birds with their vivid plumage; cooling breezes....' These early years under open skies had also given him a continuing delight in skyscapes. To their Creator he confessed the beauties and benefits of nature to be 'intimations of Thee, of how great Thou art.'

Then there are artistic and intellectual gifts. The achievements of human endeavour in agriculture, navigation, pottery, sculpture, painting, medicine, music and much more are for our comfort and delight – and all this in a fallen world under judgement. Yet these good gifts, he says, 'are merely consolations for us – for us unhappy, punished men: they are not the rewards of the blessed. What then must these be like if here in this world there are so many rich and varied gifts to enjoy?'

The vision of the City of God goes on beyond time and melts into the eternal City of God, the new Jerusalem, for which more and more Augustine yearned; 'We are really travellers all in search of the land of the happy life, the City of God.' When preaching in Carthage once and referring to the prevalent unrest, he gave expression to this longing; 'When, therefore, death shall be swallowed up in victory, these things will not be there; and there shall be peace – peace full and eternal. We shall be in a kind of city. Brethren, when I speak of that City, and especially when scandals grow great here, I just cannot bring myself to stop....'

Chapter 18

To the Land of The Happy Life

When Augustine eventually finished what he called 'this colossal book' which had so captivated his mind and imagination for thirteen years, he was over seventy and his health was broken. It was time to appoint a successor. Eraclius was chosen.

On the 26 September, 426 his congregation gathered in the Basilica of Peace to hear the bishop-elect preach. 'In this life,' Augustine told them, 'we are all bound to die; and for everyone his last day is always uncertain. Yet as babies we can look forward to being boys; and, as boys, to youth; as youths, to being grown up and, as young men, to reaching our prime and, in our prime, to growing old. Whether this will happen is not certain; but there is always something to look forward to. But an old man has no further stage of life before him. Because God wished it I came to this town in my prime: I was a young man then, now I am grown old....'

Eraclius then stepped forward to preach with the aside, 'The cricket chirps; the swan is silent.' But not for long. There was work to be done and Augustine continued preaching, advising, writing and contending. These last years were busy. He continued preaching up till his last illness while his opinion and advice continued to be sought far and wide entailing a vigorous correspondence and a constant stream of visitors.

One great concern occupied his time – his writings. Day by day he reviewed them to see whether any, especially among his earlier works, contained matter that was inconsistent with his more mature understanding of Scripture, in order that he might correct them. In 412 he had written to Marcellinus, 'If God permit me I shall gather together and point out, in a work especially devoted to this purpose, all the things which justly displease me in my books: then men shall see that I am far from being a biased judge in my own case.... For I am the sort of man who writes because he has made progress and who makes progress by writing.' These corrections came to be known as the *Retractions*. In the *Soliloquies*, written at Cassiciacum, he had commented that wisdom is not won in one way alone. Now in the *Retractions* he corrects himself: 'I was wrong in saying that more than one way led to wisdom; there is no way apart from Jesus who says, "I am the way."' In fact he retracted many statements made in that book written at the beginning of his Christian life. On looking over another work of those days, *The Immortality of the Soul,* he has to confess, 'On first reading, the reasoning is so involved and compressed as to be quite obscure. I still cannot concentrate when I read it – and I can only just make sense of it myself!'

News was daily reaching Hippo of more troubles looming. The Vandals were on the move, inexorably covering the miles through Spain and swarming across the Straits of Gibraltar into Africa. In the summer of 429 Genseric crossed over into Mauretania with his 80,000 men. He was a mere thousand miles to the west of Hippo and it seemed only a matter of time before the whole of Africa would be overrun.

Hippo was a fortified city and, as the invaders advanced, refugees made for its safety, including Possidius who described the devastation wrought by the marauding hordes, 'all armed with spears and exercised in war. They crowded the sea in ships from Spain and, passing into Africa, spread over the land, penetrating into every part of Mauretania and even into our province and district. They perpetrated all the cruelties and atrocities imaginable: robbery, murder, torture, burnings and innumerable other barbarities, so that the country became depopulated. Men took refuge in forests on the mountains or in caves among the rocks .... others were stripped and deprived of all means of subsistence and slowly perished of hunger.'

People and pastors alike looked to Augustine for guidance. To those clergy who asked whether they should flee or stay his advice was that, as long as there were Christians in need of their ministry, they should remain with their flocks. To his own people and to the refugees who had crowded into the safety of Hippo he spoke words of understanding and sympathy: 'I know you want to keep on living. You do not want to die. And you want to pass from this life to another in such a way that you will rise again, not as a dead man, but fully alive and transformed. This is what you desire. This is the deepest human feeling.' How much the martyrs must have loved the prospect of things eternal if they had so much love for the things that pass away, he mused, for they really did love this life. 'But,' he reminded them, 'with Christ death is not to be feared.'

And then the Vandals were at the gates of Hippo. By the end of May the city was under siege. Meanwhile Augustine continued preaching, counselling, reviewing – especially reviewing – as he worked in his library late on into the night.

At dinner one day as the conversation turned to the siege he confided, 'You ought to know that my prayer to God is that He will either liberate this besieged city or, if He should think otherwise, that He will give His servants strength to endure His will – or, as far as I am concerned, that He will take me from this world.' Joy and peace, he said, are the desire of all men (even of those who were at that time ravaging his homeland) for the purpose of war is peace. But the sweetness of everlasting peace belongs only to the Heavenly Jerusalem whose name signifies 'a vision of peace'.

In August he suddenly fell ill with a fever. Now that he sensed that his end was near he asked that he be left alone. Possidius recalled: 'So that his thoughts might not be distracted he asked us, about ten days before his death, to allow no one to enter his room except when the doctor came to visit or when meals were brought in.'

In keeping with his words, 'Never until the hour of his death should a Christian cease to repent,' he had those psalms of David which express penitence copied out and hung on the wall where he could read them as he poured out his heart in prayer. These words of the psalmist he could so readily make his own:

Have mercy upon me, O God,
according to Thy loving-kindness:
according unto the multitude of Thy tender
mercies
blot out my transgressions.
Wash me thoroughly from mine iniquity,
and cleanse me from my sin.
For I acknowledge my transgressions:
and my sin is ever before me.

There was also the note of yearning which throbs through so much of his own writing and which, he said, was characteristic of a Christian. Years before he had written to his friend, Paulinus: 'Do we not all long for the future Jerusalem?... I cannot refrain from this longing: I would not be human if I could. Indeed, I derive some sweetness from my very lack of self-control; and, in this sweet yearning, I seek some small consolation.' The words of another of the psalms as he read them so well expressed his mind:

> Lo, I do stretch my hands
> To Thee my help alone;
> For Thou well understands
> All my complaint and moan:
> My thirsting soul desires,
> And longeth after Thee,
> As thirsty ground requires
> With rain refreshed to be.

On 28th. August 430, in his seventy-sixth year, he died and was buried. The siege lasted another eleven months and then Hippo was evacuated. The Vandals set it on fire and moved on to take Carthage. Four years later Carthage fell and Genseric was master in Africa.

Some of the escaping bishops took Augustine's body with them and it eventually found a resting-place across the sea in Sardinia. In the eighth century the King of Lombardy had it brought to Pavia where it was buried. The shrine is in the church of San Pietro Ciel d'Oro, with the inscription:

CORPVS B P AVGVSTINI PRAESVLIS
HIPPONENSIS A PROFVCIS EPISCOPIS EX AFRICA
IN SARDINIAM DELATVM FLAVIVS
LIVTPRANDVS LONGOBARDORVM REX
A SARACENIS MAGNO PRETIO REDEMPTVM
ET SOLEMNI POMPA PAPIAM INVECTVM
IN CELEBRI BASILICA S PETRI IN COELO
AVREO DEPOSVIT ANNO REP SAL DCCXXIV[1]

Roman rule in Africa was at an end and it was not long till Christianity too disappeared under the onslaught of Arabian followers of Islam. Hippo was gradually covered over with earth and for a thousand years it was a lost city.

In the nineteenth century Algeria came under French rule and a cathedral dedicated to Augustine was built on the hill above the site of the ancient city. In 1924 excavations revealed the ruins of Augustine's church with massive paving stones on which he and his people had walked. When the French left, the area began to silt up once more.

---

1. The body of the most blessed Augustine, bishop of Hippo, brought from Africa to Sardinia by the fleeing bishops, having been purchased from the Saracens at a great price and borne with solemn pomp to Pavia, Flavius Liutprand king of the Lombards laid in the famous Basilica di San Pietro in Cielo d'Oro, in the year of the obtaining of salvation 724.

It looked as if Augustine's work was destroyed. But not so. Amazingly his library was saved and through it he has continued to speak down the ages. Thomas Aquinas, Anselm and Pascal, among others, acknowledged their debt to him as, supremely, did John Calvin – not that they agreed with all that he wrote. Luther states, 'Since the apostles' time the church has never had a better doctor than St. Augustine,' while Erasmus says simply that he was a perfect bishop!

All he had been enabled to do Augustine ascribed, after God, to his mother through whose prayers, he believed, God had given him a mind that should prefer nothing to the discovery of truth. Having found it he had used all his gifts to pass on the priceless treasure; his books, all ninety-three of them, and any other writings of interest he bequeathed to the church. He left nothing besides for he had given all his earthly goods to the poor.

Looking back to his boyhood with its energies and talents he had once written his *Deo Gratias*: 'In so small a creature what was not wonderful, not admirable? But all are gifts of my God.... Thanks to Thee, my joy, my glory, my confidence, my God, thanks to Thee for Thy gifts.' For forty years and more these gifts had been dedicated to the good of the church and rest, when it came, was welcome. 'After all His works God rested on the seventh day and the voice of His book tells us that after our works we, too, will rest with Him in the sabbath of everlasting life. The seventh day is without evening. It has no sunset.... There we shall rest and see, we shall see and love, we shall love and we shall praise. Behold what shall be in the end without end!'